# COMING TO LAS VEGAS

*A true tale of sex, drugs & Sin City in the '70s*

Carolyn V. Hamilton

*Photo credits in this book:*
*Carolyn V. Hamilton and Arthur H. Vagts*

**SWIFT HOUSE PRESS**
*Las Vegas, Nevada*

**SWIFT HOUSE PRESS**
7380 S. Eastern Avenue, Suite 124-216
Las Vegas, Nevada 89123 USA

Though every effort has been made to verify names, dates, and
places mentioned in this memoir, there may still be some
inaccuracies. No disrespect or deception is intended.

ISBN  978-0-9909664-0-1 Trade Paper Edition
Second Edition

www.carolynvhamilton.com

Cover design by Carolyn V. Hamilton

Editor, Franny Hogg Lochow

## What they're saying about *Coming to Las Vegas:*

"Carolyn V. Hamilton gives us a highly personal and quite entertaining account of her life in the Las Vegas of the 1970s. She names real names, real places, and real events. It's a nice look back on what was going on in Vegas of yesteryear. Honestly told and forthcoming. A GOOD read!"

— Peter Anthony, Las Vegas, Nevada

"*Coming to Las Vegas* is one very hot book and we're not talking Nevada weather. Hamilton gives a bar's eye view of the seamy and steamy side of America's Sin City. It's a wild ride of time, place, and opportunity and she tells the story in a most compelling and engaging fashion. It's a wow and how. Fabulous descriptions and scene-setting writing."

— Kara Knack, Malibu, California

"I thoroughly enjoy the adventure of Carolyn V. Hamilton in *Coming to Las Vegas.* The seventies were an era of change and Carolyn faced them all: drugs, alcohol, sex and women's liberation. The backdrop to her adventures was the growing city of Las Vegas and its main business, the casinos. It is interesting to see how others navigated this time of change. Great job!"

— Sue McFarlane, Spokane, Washington

"A brilliant look at behind-the-glitter Las Vegas as experienced by the ultimate insiders, the resort's cocktail servers. To them, What Happens in Vegas makes for a helluva book. Historians should make a must-read of Carolyn's work."

— David Kramer, Los Angeles, California

"This is an astonishingly good read. I defy anyone who has ever been to Las Vegas to put it down. I've been to Las Vegas many times on business, was never a gambler, so seeing these Damon Runyon types up close and personal is a revelation, even to a seasoned Vegas visitor like *moi*. If this book becomes a movie, I suggest Christina Hendricks as Carolyn."

— Jennifer Vizzo, Irving, Texas

## ACKNOWLEDGEMENTS

*Coming to Las Vegas* is dedicated to the memory of Arline Guertin, a beautiful, intelligent woman who left this world way too young.

I also wish to thank my friends and fellow MGM cocktail waitresses, who talked freely with me over the years about the things we experienced in the 70s at the MGM; my editor, Franny Hogg Lochow; and my (third) ex-husband, Cork Proctor, for creative and writing support and for continuing to laugh at all my adventures.

## INTRODUCTION

Carolyn Hamilton's memoir of her time as a Las Vegas cocktail waitress is told with uncommon candor, humor, and insight. Her stint at the world's largest hotel-casino, in a city on the verge of explosive growth and unending controversy, is a blend of Hollywood casting couch, *"2 Broke Girls,"* and *"Fear and Loathing."* It reads as fast as the characters she profiles.

Jack Sheehan,
author of "*Skin City: Uncovering the Las Vegas Sex Industry,*" and five other non-fiction books on modern Las Vegas history.

# CHAPTER TITLES

8    Carolyn V. Hamilton

*How can you tell what's real when your world moves at the speed of Vegas lights?*

## PROLOGUE – Ménage à quatre

In the hot desert night outside Lara's chintz-draped bedroom window, cicadas clatter their buzz, announcing the temperature has reached at least ninety degrees. Inside, air conditioning hums with electrical determination. Burning incense and lots of candles fill Lara's bedroom. For the night her seven-year-old daughter has been sent away to a slumber party.

Lara and Ronni and I have planned this carefully. All day we have giggled and teased Wally. Now there's champagne and naked kissing and marijuana and oral sex. He doesn't know that part of our plan is that he doesn't get to screw any of us.

Wally is a floorman in Pit One at Las Vegas' MGM Grand Hotel & Casino. Wally is safe: he's married, doesn't drink and hang out, and doesn't hit on the cocktail waitresses, so the men he works with don't see him as a pussy player. Because of this, he's sometimes called, "Weird Wally." But he lets us approach the 21, or blackjack, tables as much as we want—the more free drinks we pass out, the more tips we make—and he never complains if we're slow to bring his coffee. He's pleasant in the morning and he doesn't talk dirty. A teddy bear of a floorman, he's popular with all the cocktail waitresses.

Weird Wally is the most deserving recipient of our group favors.

Tomorrow, when the four of us go to work in the casino, it'll be business as usual. Dealers, floormen and bartenders determined to make the big sexual score will be hitting on Lara, Ronni and me—three of the forty day-shift cocktail waitresses at the MGM. If Weird Wally tells anyone what happened tonight, no one will believe him.

Which is why we picked him.

The cicadas continue their raucous buzz. In spite of the air conditioning, the air in the room is ripe with the aromas of dope and sweat and burning candle wax.

After two and a half hours of smoking and drinking and licking and fondling, we call it a night. Outside, I climb into my blue Cadillac and head home to my house near Chaparral High School. No doubt my husband, Del, who works from nine to five in law enforcement, is already asleep. Ronni's husband works swing shift in the showroom at the Aladdin, so he won't be home yet. Ronni and I will tell them we girls had a great night out, casino-hopping.

Lara lives way out on Pecos Road, a good ten-minute drive from my house. I roll down the Cadillac's windows to enjoy the night desert's pungent sage smell. It will help to clear my drink- and drug-filled head. I've taken a shower, but my mouth is as dry as a giant tumbleweed blowing across the Strip.

This has been a romp to remember. I giggle to think that poor Wally cheated on his wife and yet didn't get to really fuck. I wonder, can you call it sex if there is no penetration? Reminds me of a saying I heard when I first came to Las Vegas, "Eatin' ain't cheatin.'"

Wait a minute, what am I thinking? A wave of introspection hits me. Not guilt, exactly, but an internal questioning, nonetheless. *God, what happened to my morals?* When Ronni and Lara, two of my best friends, said this would be kicks, I didn't hesitate. And it was fun; we had a lot of laughs, mostly at Wally's expense.

Now I ask myself, how did I get to this surreal place? What's a nice Lutheran girl from Seattle doing in this crazy, upside-down world of Las Vegas?

It occurs to me that I wasn't raised to behave like such a carefree sleaze.

## CHAPTER 1 – Leaving Los Angeles

Some girls are attracted to men who are tall, dark and handsome, Latin or rich. Give me a man who can tell a great story.

That's how in Los Angeles in the fall of 1972 I came to be sitting in this out-of-the-way Mexican restaurant with fabulous food, on a first date with a man sixteen years my senior. He tells me harrowing stories of diving expeditions he's led to search for sunken treasure in the Caribbean and says, "The sea will make a Christian out of you." I notice that around his neck on a heavy chain he wears a large gold cross.

Del LaFountain has the kind of life a girl like me—hooked on the idea of adventure—would find intriguing. He has been a Drill Instructor at Paris Island, a bush pilot in Brazil, and made and lost three fortunes—he says. Now he is employed as an undercover narcotics officer for the Federal Bureau of Alcohol, Tobacco and Firearms (ATF). He drives a yellow Ford Mustang, previously confiscated in a drug bust.

I have been introduced to Del by my friend Judy, a singer and go-go dancer on the Sunset Strip.

I have just returned from a three-month backpacking trip through ten European countries and I'm suffering from the bite of the travel bug. Before that I had worked for three years as a graphic designer in a Wilshire Boulevard boutique advertising agency with interesting accounts like James B. Lansing Sound (JBL), the Canadian Rock Theater, and the Peace Corps.

I don't want to commit just yet to another serious job in advertising, so I work part-time for a new-style restaurant company called A Moveable Feast. Dressed in a long, flowered skirt, carrying a picnic-style basket, I peddle sandwiches on a route of Wilshire Boulevard offices.

Before I went to Europe, Judy tried to get me together with Del, but he was dating her boyfriend's sister. I told her, "I don't want to meet anyone who has a girl friend."

Now she has pressed, insisting, "No, no. They've broken up for good." She promised that I'd really like him. "He's an interesting guy. You'll have a lot in common."

Relationships among young people in Los Angeles in the seventies are creative, to say the least. I suspect Judy is attracted to and wants to have sex with Del herself, but her boyfriend is the jealous type. I suspect she wants me to sleep with Del and then come back and tell her what it was like. After all, what are best friends for?

Over the best flan I've ever had, Del tells me about some of his adventures with the ATF. He exudes self-confidence and his stories make me wonder and laugh. He finishes dinner with a pipe-bowl of Borkhum Riff. While I'm not a fan of cigarette smoke, I like the smell of his tobacco, and I admit, I am attracted.

One of the businesses Del has made and lost was a Las Vegas corporation called Continental Property Management. "I sold it to my accountant and went down to Brazil to become a bush pilot," he tells me. "A year later, I came back for my first annual payment, the guy took me out to his backyard at a barbecue and confessed he'd embezzled money and the business was broke. The IRS offered to give me back the business, but I was burned out, so I just went back to Brazil."

Del tells me about his ATF friends and others in Las Vegas. He's even had a date with Ann Margret. He loves Las Vegas. With a knowing smile he says, "It's a great town when you're connected."

I feel like I have met a true soldier-of-fortune, complete with rugged tan, wiry build, sporty mustache and fascinating stories. A girl might listen skeptically to adventurous tales told by a man newly met, but Judy has known Del for seven years.

By Christmas Del and I are an item, planning future travels together.

I'm in love.

One day he tells me about some Latin friends who work in Las Vegas and want him to join them in a new business.

"What kind of business?" I ask.

"A circus."

He explains that these friends have a trapeze act called The Flying Farfans, and they plan to leave Circus Circus, the hotel/casino where they currently perform, at the end of their five-year contract.

"They're tired of working for someone else and want to start their own business," he says. "They want me to be their general manager. I think it's just because of the government connections they think I have. Most circus families come from other countries and have ongoing problems with immigration. Because in their home countries you need friends in high places, they think it works the same way in America."

"Does this new business have a name?" I ask.

"They're going to call it The Las Vegas International Circus."

What could be more adventurous than a circus? I am smitten with Del and smitten with the romantic idea of joining a circus. Forget about my promising future in Los Angeles advertising as a graphic designer and peddling sandwiches on Wilshire Boulevard. How soon can we leave?

## CHAPTER 2 – Coming to Las Vegas

Del takes a leave of absence from his ATF job. He goes to a banker friend and with a handshake arranges a loan on a new trailer, a 28-foot Wilderness.

"You're crazy to think you can pull that trailer with a '64 Mustang," his friend the banker tells him.

One of the things that attracts me to Del is that he's the do-it kind of guy whose instinctive response is, "Oh yeah? Watch me!" He says somebody's always telling him he can't do something. "That's when I just go out and do it."

Del says there's no rush to drive to Las Vegas and get involved in the new circus business because the Farfans' contract isn't quite up yet.

"Let's take a vacation," he says. "Let's drive down to Baja and chill on the beach. We'll watch great sunsets, drink *cervezas* and eat fresh shrimp that's just been hauled in."

Yes.

Del in San Felipe

With that Mustang, Del hauls the Wilderness down to San Felipe, on the Sea of Cortez side of Baja. San Felipe is a quiet little Mexican fishing village, warm, sunny, kind of barren. The Sea of Cortez spreads from horizon to horizon. After ten days of walking the beach, hanging out with a few gringos, drinking beer and stuffing ourselves on shrimp, we head back north and up into the high desert of southern Nevada.

On March 31, 1973, after the Mexican vacation, Del and I pull into Las Vegas. He stops at 3794 Las Vegas Boulevard South, to drive into the Lone Palm Motel and Trailer Park. This is the northwest corner of Tropicana and the famous Las Vegas Strip— just south of a Union 76 gas station with a sign in front that says, "Free Aspirin and Tender Sympathy."

"I've stayed here when I worked undercover drug deals out of Vegas," Del tells me. "The managers are friends of mine so we'll get a good rate."

Indeed we are warmly welcomed by The Lone Palm managers Bill and Joanne. Inside the air-conditioned office, Bill asks, "How long will you stay this time?"

"I'm on a leave-of-absence from the feds," Del says, "and looking at a business deal. We'll probably be here a few months."

Bill says, "I'm sorry we don't have a parking spot available in the permanent section, but you can park your trailer in the gravel area." While the permanent section is shaded by big, leafy trees, the gravel area is a huge, open piece of acreage between the motel and Tropicana Avenue. Bill is delighted that we'll be around for awhile.

The next day I take time to walk around the trailer park and this open, barren area where we're parked. It is April 1 and already the mid-day temperature is in the nineties, the air heavy to breathe.

The Tropicana Hotel & Casino

The front door of our trailer faces the tallest thing I see: on the opposite corner in front of the Tropicana Hotel is a big white, crown-shaped, fountain-inspired statue. This hotel bills itself as, "The Tiffany of Las Vegas."

Behind the trailers in the open area, a wide expanse of gravel ends at the edge of the Dunes Emerald Greens Golf and Country Club.

North of our trailer, behind some scrubby oleander bushes, are the taxi-cab yellow, cinderblock office and motel rooms of The Lone Palm. The other side of the office is where the tree-shaded rows of permanent trailers rest. In a separate building are washers and dryers, toilets and showers. Between the office and the Strip, a grassy area with a swimming pool and children's playground is shaded by a row of Chinese Elms that stretch to the sidewalk.

The Lone Palm advertises, "116 luxurious trailer spaces." Maybe back among the trees, but not out here in the gravel where we're parked.

Over free coffee in Bill's office, Del tells me, "You'll meet a lot of circus people here. They like to stay here because it's cheap and they can keep animals in portable cages out back."

*Oh boy*, I think, *this is really going to be exciting.*

At the back of The Lone Palm property there's a hole in the Dunes Golf Course chain link fence. I discover I can get onto the golf course while the day is still cool for an early walk.

When I return I find several people gathered behind our trailer, squinting in the morning sun. They are here to watch a circus performer work with his trained lions. The day before I hadn't noticed this big cage because of the trailers parked around it. Now it's alive with snarling cats and a short guy with a shock of blond hair and a whip.

I walk over to where Del stands, leaning in the shade against one of the trailers, smoking his pipe.

"How can those cats stand this heat?" I ask. "They're probably growling for air-conditioning."

Del laughs and puts his arm around me. "Lions are from Africa."

"Oh. Well. Guess they're used to it."

\* \* \*

In April, 1973 I stand on the sidewalk of the famous Las Vegas Strip and brace myself against the strong desert winds that blow tumbleweeds across the street.

*Good Lord*, I think, *what a windblown, brown wasteland.*

If the desert winds of April didn't swirl sand everywhere, beautiful mountain views on all sides would be visible. Tumbleweeds compete with cars in a crazy dance on the wide Strip. I hate these high winds because I wear hard contact lenses. To walk from the car to the trailer or from the office to the washing machine I have to peek through the fingers of my cupped hands.

A few years ago, in the sixties, I spent two different weekends in Las Vegas partying, which may explain why I don't remember all this yukky wind and blowing sand.

I can't believe how dry the air is. The balls of my feet harden so fast that the skin splits. For two days the pain is like walking on paper cuts. When I brush my hair it stands up and crackles with electricity. This is a climate for picking your nose. Things crust up in there so often that I'm afraid if I stay here I'll develop the habit. I go through a lot of rewetting drops for my contacts.

"How can anyone live here?" I ask Del.

"You get used to it. Besides, it's not like we're staying long. We'll be going on the road."

Can't be soon enough for me. Still, I wonder, what is it that attracts people to move here? To have a house or apartment, a job, and go to work every day?

This feels to me like a temporary town, not someplace you'd ever call "home." It looks like a pass-through for people born somewhere else, on their way to somewhere else. A bus stop in the desert.

I have the impression that here the fast buck rules, and excitement comes from the feeling that you're on the "last frontier." You feel like anything is possible here—the big score, the instant fame. Everyone's seen *Ocean's Eleven* and heard of the infamous Rat Pack.

Lots of entry-level jobs beckon, with the idea that once you get a foot in the door, big, breath-taking things will happen. Who thinks about what it will be like here twenty years from now? No one I know considers buying an acre off the Strip for $2,500 and sitting on it for thirty years to make a million dollars.

Everyone but me seems to love the weather. Joanne justifies the high temperatures with a phrase I will hear again and again: "But it's a *dry* heat." Still, when it's upwards of a hundred, people hide behind their air conditioners. I'm amazed that our little generator can cool the interior of the Wilderness trailer.

Del enjoys hanging out in The Lone Palm office drinking coffee and swapping stories with Bill, who spends his evenings listening to the police radio. I get the impression that Bill lives another life vicariously through Del.

These guys can talk for hours with nostalgia for "the good old days when the mob ruled the town." Apparently it was great—unless you were black.

Then you had to stay on the West Side "with your own kind", even if you were a star like Sammy Davis, Jr.

* * *

I think Bill and Joanne are about the same age as Del, in their mid-forties. For ten years they have had the run of The Lone Palm. Joanne wears her bleached-white hair in a bubble *a la* 1959 and sleeps every day until noon. Bill, a man with dark bushy eyebrows, white sideburns and a quiet voice, also runs an under-the-table business. He buys and sells televisions and guns and used appliances and this and that.

Since they came to The Lone Palm from Oklahoma, Bill and Joanne have never taken a vacation.

"Do you think he's cooking the books?" I ask Del. I can imagine how, in Bill's management capacity, this would be easy to do. "They take in so much cash. Why else would they never want to take a vacation?"

Del tamps tobacco into his pipe bowl before he answers. "I'm not saying it's true, but a vacation could mean a sudden increase in Lone Palm profits that the property owner would notice."

The following Monday, Neil Griffin arrives and Del introduces me. Neil, who was Del's long-time ATF boss, lives at The Lone Palm during the week. On the weekends he drives home to Orange County. In his off hours, Neil likes to hang out in The Lone Palm office, too. I learn that Neil, Del and Bill love to drink coffee together, reminisce about "the old days" and share off-color racist and gender-insensitive jokes.

During our first week at The Lone Palm I begin to meet some of the "regulars."

One afternoon we're hanging around the office drinking coffee when in walks a hippie-looking guy about my age wearing a cowboy hat. Kind of a nice-looking guy, I think.

"This is John," Bill says. "He lives here."

"Just dropped in to get my mail," John says. "Gotta head over to the West Side before dark to find a guy."

Bill hands him some envelopes. "Nice t'meetcha," John says, tips a finger to his hat, and leaves.

"What does he do?" I ask Del.

Del looks at Bill who looks at Neil and the three of them laugh.

"That's John, the bounty-hunter," Bill says. "He makes money finding guys for a bail-bondsman."

Who knew there were real bounty hunters today? I remember bounty hunters as characters in old westerns.

Neil watches John get into his car. "We think on the side he also deals a little dope and pimps a little pussy."

Bill follows his gaze and smiles. "Live and let live."

Next afternoon I'm in the office talking to Joanne when a car pulls up in front. "Bill," Joanne calls. "Helen's here."

Bill comes to the front of the desk, carrying some little electronic gadget he's in the middle of repairing. I stand to one side to let a skinny, wrinkled woman who looks older than she probably is open the office door. A blast of hot air enters with her. She approaches the desk. She doesn't say anything as she gives Bill some crumpled bills. He hands her a key. She nods and leaves, banging the door behind her. No paperwork.

"We think she lives out of that old car," Joanne confides. "Or maybe she just uses it for storage."

I peek out the window to look as the woman gets into her car. Junk is packed so high in the back seat and on the passenger side of the front seat that when she drives she can't possibly see out of any of those windows. I would be afraid to drive a car like that.

Every time Helen leaves and comes back, her car looks exactly the same, as if none of the stuff has ever been moved. I am amazed the police don't stop her while she's driving.

A few hours later Mack arrives. Bill introduces us, and asks if we'd like to buy some jumbo prawns at a good price?

"Got good packets of big frozen ones," Mack says. "Just off the plane from Mexico."

We all go outside to Mack's car. Mack opens the trunk. It is stuffed with cardboard boxes.

"Twenty-five cents a pound," Mack says.

Bill and Joanne buy three boxes and we buy one.

Over a delicious prawn dinner that evening in the tiny kitchen of our trailer, Del explains, "There's a huge black market in Vegas for shrimp and lobsters from Mexico. They come in the same way the drugs come in—small planes flying so low over the Salton Sea that they're under the government's radar. Then they land somewhere close in the desert, and the goods are distributed around town through a pre-established network."

I guess Bill is a part of the "network." While the feds are quite interested in drugs, I get the impression they're not too concerned about illegal seafood.

On weekends the Lone Palm is always full. The weekenders spend most of their time at the pool yelling at their kids. The intense heat and desert winds don't seem to bother them at all.

Because of the variety of people who pass through The Lone Palm, I begin to refer to the motel as, "The crossroads of the world."

In a letter to my parents in Seattle I write, *"There are not a lot of rules here; in addition to children and dogs and cats it's not uncommon to see lions, chimpanzees, or even an elephant. This may not be a very intellectually-stimulating place to live, but it certainly is colorful!"*

## CHAPTER 3 – Circus Circus

This morning over coffee Del says, "Today we're going out to meet Carlos." I've been looking forward to meeting this man I've heard so much about.

We lock the trailer and climb into the yellow Mustang. Del drives east on Flamingo Road. From the Strip to Maryland Parkway—about a mile—single-story, flat-roofed bars, shops, restaurants, and the occasional convenience store and laundromat pepper both sides of the street.

At a traffic signal at Maryland Parkway, the four lanes abruptly end and create a bottleneck of traffic because continuing east, the road is now two lanes.

Early in the morning this congestion makes me think for a minute that I'm back in L.A. We pass Eastern Avenue, with its new traffic signal, and the desert expands on either side. Not a tree to mar the view. Here and there I note a lone new house or bar.

Del drives with one hand on the wheel and his left elbow resting out the window. He tells me that the Farfans are among the first aerialists to perform, in 1968, at Circus Circus. "Carlos and his brother, Armando, are from Santiago, Chile. In their family, circus performing goes back four generations on their father's side. Five generations on their mother's side."

At Pearl Street we turn onto a macadam road with no sidewalks. A few lots contain houses under construction. Not a palm tree or oleander or pampas grass has yet been planted. After living my entire life so far in Seattle, Detroit, and Los Angeles, this is like another planet.

We pull into the driveway of a large two-story, beige stucco house with a red tile roof. This is where the Farfans live, together with various relatives and children.

As we're getting out of the car, Carlos comes out the front door. "Del, *mi amigo!*"

Del introduces me. "This is my girl friend, Carolyn. She does advertising and public relations."

When Carlos Farfan smiles, deep vertical dimples crease his tanned cheeks. The catcher in the Flying Farfans trapeze act, he is a handsome, dyed-blond hulk. He is also acting head of a large, familial group that includes his younger brother Armando and Armando's Czechoslovakian wife, Anna.

Carlos takes my hand and graciously plants a kiss. "*Muy bonita*," he murmurs. The size of his hand makes me think of a baseball catcher's mitt.

Carlos leads us around the side of the big house. In the desert-scraped backyard stand two complete trapeze structures: one adult-size, and a smaller version for children. He introduces me to some family, some friends.

The adults wear an abundance of heavy gold rings, necklaces, bracelets and watches. The children raise dust in the yard as they run laughing and screaming, chased by several ratty-looking dyed pink poodles.

At the back of the house Carlos opens a sliding glass door and takes us inside. The large living room contains bulky, well-lived-with furniture. Children's toys and dog toys litter the wall-to-wall carpet. We sit on a blue brocade sofa and Carlos directs a pretty, teen-aged girl to bring us coffee. She leaves the room and another woman enters.

"Carolina, this is my wife, Theresa. She is one of The Flying Farfans," Carlos says.

"*Mucho gusto*, Carolina." Theresa is Peruvian, with straight dark hair, intense brown eyes and a stocky build that doesn't look like it would be aerodynamically easy to fly. As we chat, I decide that Theresa has a warm personality, but even when she smiles I sense about her an aura of determination.

The girl brings a tray with coffee, cream, spoons and a big bowl of sugar. Theresa pours a cup for me and confides, "I learned the trapeze to work with my husband so I can keep an eye on him."

Del pours his own coffee, adding a lot of cream. "The Flying Farfans worked with Ringling Brothers and Barnum & Bailey," he says to me. "They've been doing five shows a day at Circus Circus for five years."

Carlos grins, revealing handsome, even teeth. "And soon we will have our own business. You must come tomorrow and see the show."

* * *

The next day at noon Del and I arrive at the Circus Circus Hotel Casino to see The Flying Farfans perform.

The first thing I notice are the grotesque, larger-than-life white sculptures of gorillas, lions, elephants and clowns that face the Strip sidewalk. Behind them rows of fountains front Circus Circus, where a three-story, white and hot pink-striped canopy dominates the *porte cochère.*

At the hotel entrance a bustle of cars and taxis move slowly in and out of several lanes. As we wait our turn for valet parking, Del says, "That pink was the idea of the marketing director, Mel Larson. To promote Circus Circus, he even wears pink suits and drives a pink Cadillac."

This makes me laugh. "Crazy," I say. "But it's a good visual signature."

Carlos

Theresa

## The Flying Farfans

"Also this is the first hotel/casino in Vegas to welcome the middle-American family market. They have the largest permanent circus in the world in here."

We get out of the Mustang and Del hands the keys to the valet attendant in exchange for a claim ticket. As we enter the casino he tells me about the Chairman of the board Bill Bennett and his partner Bill Pennington.

"They've led a new trend in Vegas—they took their company public and awakened Wall Street to gambling investments." Del smiles. "Bennett hates that pink, but his business instinct can't argue with its success."

We enter the casino "midway" and I look up to see that the Flying Farfans' trapeze dominates the tent-shaped ceiling. From the Dice Pit and blackjack tables and slot machines players can gaze upwards at the entertainment while they gamble. Del leads me into an elevator and we descend to a level that contains a maze of hallways and offices. We catch up with Carlos, Theresa, Armando and Anna in their dressing room.

Theresa pulls on flesh-colored fishnet stockings peppered with dime-sized orange rhinestones and talks about the art of the trapeze. She shakes her head and says, "I do not understand. The Passing Leap is more difficult to execute than the Triple Somersault, but the Triple gets more applause."

"Appearances are everything," I say.

In the hallway I am introduced to three dark-haired girls in scanty, candy-colored clown costumes. Theresa cheek-kisses the girls. "They toss balloons down into the casino," she says. "They ride horses hanging from the monorail in the ceiling. Their act is called The Clown Carousel." I wonder, are the casino owners hoping the players will be so distracted they can't help but lose at the tables?

Besides the sounds of slot machines and screams of children and excited gamblers, the casino reverberates with the Hammond B3 organ that is the centerpiece of a live band that accompanies the performers. The booming amplified voices of alternating ringmasters Mike Hartzell, Clarence Hoffman and Tommy Rundell announce each act with true circus ballyhoo. I can feel the excitement induced by this cacophony of sound, and I like it.

Acts that alternately appear with the Farfans from noon to midnight include the Berosini Jungle Fantasy with Bobby Berosini and his orangutans. Bobby Berosini is the brother of Armando's wife, Anna. There are some Hungarian acrobats called The Seven Endress. Simona Prince is an athletic young woman who performs her solo act in a spangled bikini and top hat as she hangs by her teeth with no safety net from a trapeze that circles slowly on the casino ceiling's monorail.

Simona, who is also one of the three Clown Carousel girls, tells me, "The cocktail waitresses hate Bobby's orangutans. They all have to go up and down in the same elevator from the dressing rooms and the orangutans stink."

Lilian is a Czechoslovakian performer who juggles with her feet. There is an act simply called Tanya the Elephant. Tanya would later become the most famous elephant in Las Vegas, playing Keno and slot machines and appearing on television and in film. Armando's blond wife not only flies with the Farfans but has a dog act called Miss Anna's Oodles of Poodles. They are the same pink-dyed poodles I'd seen at the house. Del hates them. "Those damn yappy poodles overrun the house."

The ceiling monorail is also used by five girls who hang and twist and pose in an aerial ballet.

* * *

In the foyer of the Pearl house, Carlos looks me up and down and says, "You must be in our aerial ballet." I'm not sure if he's asking, or declaring.

From a business standpoint, it is cost-effective for every circus member to have more than one skill. "I will also make a solo act for you," he says. So in addition to doing advance public relations, I will be a real circus performer.

Interestingly, Carlos does not ask Del to do anything other than "manage the business."

By the end of my second week in Las Vegas, I'm going every day to the house where the aerial ballet girls rehearse. All the moves are choreographed, practiced and perfected on the ground before moving into the air. I find this to be much more gymnastic than ballet. I complain to Del, "As a kid I loved studying ballet, but I hated gym. I never saw myself as an athletic person."

My challenge is that at five-feet-ten-inches I am five inches taller—and twenty pounds heavier—than any of the other girls. Who can pull all that weight up off the ground? Not me. What is Carlos thinking?

My first epiphany: circus performers are smaller than me.

On Friday Carlos shows me a thirty-five foot pole and points to the top. I crane my neck to see the tiny platform way up there.

"You pose on the platform, then dive like a swan and slide upside down to the ground, where I catch you." Carlos says this with a sincere smile, though I bet he's laughing inside at the stunned look on my face.

I mumble my response. "Sure."

"Armando will go up with you to show you. There is a safety belt he will put around your waist."

Wonderful.

Armando and I climb a narrow rope ladder to the platform. At the top of the pole, the platform seems just as small as it looked from the ground. Armando helps me to stand on shaky legs. He directs me to raise my arms so he can attach the safety belt around my waist. "Very safe," he assures me.

I know they say, *don't look down*, but I don't see how to avoid it. Below, Carlos, Theresa, Del, the aerial ballet girls and several children make up a critical—to my point of view—audience. I'm aware of my heart thumping. I'm desperate to back out, but I don't want to lose face. If they think I can do this, maybe I can.

Armando clicks the hook from the safety belt to a metal piece on the finger-thick guy wire. This wire stretches in a forty-five degree angle from the top of the pole to the ground. This is the wire that I will zip down.

Oh. My. God.

Armando shows me the heavy, stuffed cloth loop that attaches to the wire. The idea is that I will zip down this wire upside down in my swan-like dive, hanging by one looped ankle.

I am so terrified I forget to breathe. My mother's face flashes in front of me. If she knew I was doing this, she'd faint. Armando, all business, doesn't seem to notice my distress. He unhooks the loop so that it's loose on the wire, takes my right foot in his hand, and slides the loop over the heel and up to my ankle.

He guides me to sit down on the platform and shows me how to position my body for the dive. No standing, statuesque, pre-dive pose yet—this first time I will leap from a sitting position.

Armando touches the top of my hand. "You must let go of the pole."

Fear pours out of me in the sweat streaming from my palms. My hands are too slippery anyway to hang onto the pole.

A rush of air—I scream—it's over.

In Carlos' arms I open my eyes. I don't even remember squeezing them shut. My heart pounds so hard my chest hurts and I can't catch my breath.

Everyone gathers around me with words of encouragement. Theresa waves a stocky hand and laughs. "No, no, Carolina," she says. "You must keep your *eyes* open and your *mouth* closed, not the other way."

* * *

At the end of June, 1974 I turn thirty, the magic age after which the hippies say nobody is to be trusted. Del, Bill, Joanne and Neil present me with a chocolate birthday cake, decorated with two pink frosting roses and lettering that reads, "Happy Birthday to Over-The-Hill."

In the evening Del takes me to the Clark County Library on Flamingo Road to watch a free movie. Summer nights in the desert are the most pleasant time of day. By 9 p.m. the temperature drops about twenty degrees and the air smells like dry sage.

Tonight the library is projecting the 1969 folk/rock music festival *Woodstock* on the big south wall of the library building. Blanket-to-blanket Las Vegans sit on the grass enjoying a perfect summer evening.

Of course, I've already seen *Woodstock* twice. I'm thinking this is a great opportunity to introduce "my" music to my older man. Del is not impressed. He gives me an indulgent smile, shakes his head and says, "Movie about a bunch of druggies."

The next day, Del takes me out for our favorite lunch: the Caesar salad in the coffee shop at the Stardust. I've read that this two-story hotel/casino has forty acres of gardens and an electric sign that their PR people claim is the largest of its kind in the world. With 7,100 feet of neon tubing, 32,000 feet of wiring and 41,000 light bulbs, they might be right. They also claim the sign is visible from three miles out in the desert. In Vegas, everyone loves numbers.

The Stardust Hotel & Casino

We have developed a routine where we go for the tasty Caesar salad and afterwards play a couple of hands of blackjack to see if we can cover the cost of the lunch. Del has taught me how to play the game, how to pick the best table—and the best seat at that table—to play, and the best time of day to play. And he warns me not to get too excited about it.

Then we go over to Circus—I've learned no one in town ever uses both words to refer to Circus Circus—to hang out with the Farfans and catch up on the latest familial and circus gossip.

As we approach the hotel, I notice that a prankster has painted the balls on the big white gorilla red.

Today Theresa tells me that Olga, one of the Peruvian aerial ballet girls who also lives in a trailer at The Lone Palm, has had sex with Jay Sarno. Theresa is disgusted. "She did it for a bag of groceries."

I've seen the fat Jay Sarno around the hotel. He was pointed out to me as the large-living, casino mogul who was the mind behind Caesars Palace and Circus Circus. Del says, "He's the father of the fantasy resort concept."

Our aerial ballet girl, Olga, works as a change girl at Circus while we all wait for the Las Vegas International Circus to get organized and ready to go on the road.

"She did it for a bag of groceries?"

"Change girls do not make much money," Theresa says. "Let's go play bingo."

Theresa loves bingo. Circus doesn't have a bingo parlor, and even if it did, the big hotels all have rules forbidding employees to drink and gamble where they work. Her favorite games are down the street at the Riviera. The Flying Farfans have a forty-minute break between shows and that's when she likes to play.

"Come on," she says, happy at the prospect of a bingo companion. "We have to hurry."

She throws a long cotton shirt over her costume and slips into flat shoes. I follow her out to her car and we jump in. We don't wait for the air conditioning to cool down the interior inferno. Theresa speeds down the strip with the same focus she used to learn to fly so she could keep an eye on Carlos.

At the Riviera we are lucky to find a parking space on the shady side of the building. We leave the car by an unmarked side door and run inside. We play several games of bingo. Theresa has everything timed. She knows exactly when to stop so we can run down the hallway to the door, get in the car, drive back to Circus, and arrive five minutes before their next show. I am impressed. I don't think it ever occurs to her that she could be late.

\* \* \*

The stifling heat of the high desert summer has set in. I have given up any thoughts of being a circus performer. I have no ambition to do anything. The trailer's air conditioning also seems tired because it is not doing its job.

I'm hot, I'm depressed, I feel bloated, and I'm bored.

In another letter to my parents I write:

*"How can I describe the desert? It's unbelievable. Every day the temperature rises above 100 degrees. When the wind blows there is sand everywhere. The water comes out of the tap hot. There are big bugs in the trees that buzz continuously in the heat. There has been a plague of water beetles—that look like cockroaches to me—and butterflies, due to this year's extreme heavy spring rains. Southern Nevada is Las Vegas. Outside this city is nothing but desert. The only other city anyone's ever heard of is Reno, up by Lake Tahoe. It's even smaller than Las Vegas, if that's possible. This town is a cultural wasteland. If you don't gamble or drink or play golf, there's nothing to do. In the summer it's too hot to do anything outside, even lie in the sun. I'm surprised more of these bald old men aren't found on the golf courses dead of a heat stroke. Las Vegas simply has no class whatsoever. What price, adventure? As you may have guessed by now, I can't wait to get out of here!"*

\* \* \*

The days continue to drag. Nothing is *happening*. Still in culture shock, I feel suffocated. I tell myself it is only a lull, but I am consumed with impatience. I hate waiting.

Carlos has gone to Central America to book the Las Vegas International Circus for the coming winter season, beginning November 1.

"He's already booked twenty-two weeks in El Salvador and Guatemala alone," announces Theresa with pride.

She and I are drinking *café au laits* and eating chocolate croissants at Andre's French Bakery, a new café in a tiny storefront on Maryland Parkway. Carlos brought Del and me here a few months ago and introduced us to the owner, Andre Rochat. This is the only place in town where you can sit outside at little round tables—if you can stand the heat.

We are sitting inside, where there is refreshing air-conditioning. I sip my *café au lait* and say, "I had no idea the circus was such big business in Central America."

"Oh yes, the governments of the countries will provide all transportation, advertising, and accommodations." She breaks her chocolate croissant in half. "They will collect all the money, the gate receipts, pay all the performers a weekly salary, and present Carlos, as the circus owner, with the rest of the money before we leave the country."

"Naturally, the government takes their cut first."

"Oh, yes, of course." Theresa's tone is now more resigned than proud.

We leave Andre's French Bakery for home, each with a brown paper bag of pastries to go. I drive back to The Lone Palm, thinking that Central American countries have a strange way of doing business. However, this booking information is exciting news. Winter looks promising for our circus adventure.

I park the Mustang in front of The Lone Palm office so I can check for mail. The leaves of the Chinese elms barely move in the hot air. Winter seems like a looooong way off. This getting ready to take the show on the road has taken more time than Del and I had planned, and we don't get paid until the circus goes to work.

We are eager for November to come. We are running out of money.

## CHAPTER 4 – The amazing world of Vegas advertising

When June arrives, I decide I can't sit around any more. I have to go to work. In a town of 175,000 people, I am afraid there won't be a lot of jobs for graphic designers. With my slick Los Angeles portfolio full of ads for clients like JBL Sound, Great Western Savings and The Peace Corps, I get interviews at all four major ad agencies.

I am thrilled to be hired by Bob Brown, a balding partner at May Advertising. He gives me the title, Associate Art Director.

I am thrilled to have scored big time here. May Advertising is the largest advertising agency in Nevada. The offices are in a one-story building practically tucked under the Sahara Avenue overpass, on Industrial Road—the name taken from the area's automotive, printing, tire, and manufacturing businesses.

Glamorous ad agency, not so glamorous neighborhood.

"You're overqualified to be just a graphic designer," Bob Brown tells me, adjusting his glasses with one finger, "and I can't hire you as Art Director, so Associate is the best I can do."

He goes on to explain that Ed Felesky, the present art director, really doesn't want the job, which is why he regularly indulges in two-martini lunches. But Ed plays golf with Bob's partner Jerry May, and Jerry insisted that Ed should be head of the art department. My first introduction to personal connections called "Vegas juice."

The third partner is Jim Joyce. At six-feet-three inches, thirty-four-year-old Joyce towers over just about everybody. Like a lot of people who aren't comfortable with their height, he slumps his shoulders in a way that turns his body into a question mark. He lives politics and with all that shmoozing attracts most of the agency's political clients. He is away from the agency a lot, usually up in Nevada's state capitol, Carson City.

After hiring me, I don't see much of Bob Brown. He also owns the *Valley Times* and another newspaper up in Lacey, Washington, so he too is often out of town.

Jerry May, for whom the agency is named, is a short, rotund man with thin blond hair. His personality is outgoing in a good-old-boy fashion. In general, Brown and Joyce leave the day-to-day management of the agency to him.

In addition to Art Director Ed Felesky and me, there are three other graphic designers, Billy Vasiliadis, John Dykema, and a white-haired gentleman who designs only full-page newspaper car ads.

Bob told me that in the art department I can do whatever I want, and the first thing I want to do is to get them organized. There is no job-numbering system, nobody knows what the other artists are working on, and jobs are billed according to what the agency owners think the client will pay.

"How does that work, exactly?" I ask Ed.

Ed is maybe in his late 40s or early 50s, has a quiet voice and moves slowly. He shrugs his shoulders and grins. His face has the vacant look of someone not-in-the-here-and-now. I decide it's not a productive idea to ask him any questions right after lunch.

I set up a numbering system by job and an hourly tracking and accounting system for everyone in the art department. None of the guys object, since I do all the paperwork.

It is the height of the campaign season, and twenty-two political clients keep our art department busy. We churn out political brochures, bumper stickers and newspaper ads in a hurry with no strategic campaign information and little creative thought. An ad for one guy running for county commission looks just like the ad for the other guy running for county commission. And why doesn't somebody tell Hank Thornley to lose the pencil-thin mustache? Who will vote for a political candidate who looks like a 1920s snake oil salesman?

I worked in Los Angeles. I think I know it all.

In the Los Angeles world of advertising having more than one client in the same business is considered a blatant conflict of interest. Not in Nevada. In addition to the political clients, May Advertising handles several hotel/casinos, including the recently opened downtown Union Plaza.

"Yeah, we created over two hundred logos for the owner, Jackie Gaughan," Ed tells me. Is that a hint of pride I hear in his voice?

John Dykema nods and says, "He finally picked one at the last minute because the Plaza was opening and he couldn't wait any longer for the print stuff."

Two hundred and fifty logo designs? Cost-effective? I don't think so.

The Union Plaza has a showroom where they plan to bring in the musical *South Pacific*. May Advertising will design the show's billboards and ads. All the artists work on this. I am the only one who builds into the title of the design a reclining, nude native girl with a big white flower strategically located at her crotch.

My instinct that T&A sells big here in Las Vegas turns out to be right on. Joy Hamman, who does the Plaza's publicity, takes all our designs to the big bosses, and they pick mine. That Friday, my *South Pacific* ad appears in the entertainment newspaper, *Panorama*. Publisher Ralph Petillo claims his little 56-page weekly tabloid is "Nevada's largest circulated newspaper."

My South Pacific billboard design

Del and I get to see for free the opening performance of *South Pacific*. I have seen both the play and the movie and I am shocked by this production.

In the dark of the showroom I whisper to Del, "Whole scenes are gone! This is crazy." The script has been rewritten to focus on that T&A. It also has been shortened considerably so that people will not be too tired at the end of the show to return to gambling in the casino.

When I was in my high school drama department, we had to get all kinds of permissions to produce a Broadway show. There are legalities here—I'm not sure what they are—but I'm pretty sure you can't legally change so radically the content of *South Pacific*.

In a *Panorama* article on the page before the adult pull-out section, *South Pacific* producer Maynard Sloate explains why he put young Scott Stewart in the role of Emile de Becque: "It struck us that there would be broader audience appeal if we had a more youthful actor in the role." Like Sloate can improve on *South Pacific*. Give me a break.

"How can they get away with that?" I ask Joy. I like Joy a lot; she's a former showgirl turned publicist who reminds me of what Ava Gardner might look like after a lifetime of buffets. Joy has a quick wit and is outspoken.

She laughs and says, "Honey, don't you worry about it. This is Vegas."

Just some of many surprises for the young designer from the Wilshire Boulevard ad agency with the L.A. standards who knows it all.

I may be righteous and indignant, but my choices are to adapt to the way this business works in Vegas, or quit.

Still, I take the work seriously. How do I figure out how to show the guys—I'm the only woman in the art department— tactfully how to produce better quality work? I can't tell them I think what they are doing is shlock. One thing I've already learned is that in Vegas nobody wants to hear "how it's done in L.A." At Williams Costume, where Theresa and Anna buy rhinestones, sequins, feathers and fishnets, there is a sign on the wall behind the cash register that says in big, block letters, "We don't care how they do it in L.A."

* * *

My job at May Advertising does have great benefits. Besides being just ten minutes from the Lone Palm, my salary is higher than it was in L.A., and I get to wear jeans to work. The other women in the agency are young and pretty. They wear a lot of make-up, cutesy dresses, false hair, false eyelashes and pantyhose—in 100-degree heat. When did I step into a 1950s car ad?

One day, the office manager, Jean, comes to the art department to see me. Every hair is regimentally tucked into Jean's French twist. She wears a crisp, cotton shirtdress cinched at the waist with a pink patent leather belt.

"We have a KP system for all the coffee cups," she says. "We put our names on a list, and for a week one girl goes around to all the offices at the end of the day, picks up the coffee cups, washes them and cleans up the coffee area. That way none of us has to do it very often. I'm adding your name to the list."

This seems reasonable. "The art department would be happy to participate," I say with a smile.

"No, you don't understand." Jean shakes her tidy head. "Only the girls do it. Not the guys."

"I see."

This seems to pacify her, and she returns to her office.

Miffed at the sexual inequality of how this clean-up task is accomplished, I tell my fellow artists that we all should participate in the KP list, and couldn't I add their names, too?

Ed Felesky blinks and smiles—he's leaving shortly for his martini lunch. Billy Vasiliadis and John Dykema stare at me as if I'd just suggested they donate their balls to science. The car guy never raises his head from his drafting board and the ad he's laying out. Ed, Billy and John laugh out loud. The car guy smirks. I can see that where the men are concerned the coffee-cup-washing subject is not on their planet.

I go to see Jean in her office, where she's surrounded by potted plants, stacks of magazines and framed family photos.

"I'm sorry," I say, "but I won't be participating in the KP list. The art department voted against it."

"What are you talking about?" Her black-lined eyes narrow. "Voted? They don't have to vote. They don't have anything to do with this."

"Well, yeah, they do." I take my sixties liberation stand. "I see myself as part of the art department, not part of a group of women who work here. I'd be happy to wash coffee cups, but only if the men participate in the system, too. I think that's fair. But I guess the guys don't want to do it, because they voted against it."

Jean glares at me with hostile eyes. Apparently no one before has ever challenged her office authority.

"I *have* to wash coffee cups," she declares. "All the women do it, and you will, too." She threatens to "take this straight to the president of the company."

Jerry May is out of town, so three days go by while Jean and I pass each other in the hallway and coffee room without speaking.

The afternoon of the day Jerry returns, I look up from my drafting table to see him standing in front of me, his bulk blocking my vision of the rest of the room. He is wearing a purple jumpsuit with a white patent-leather belt and white patent-leather shoes. I think of a Fruit-of-the-Loom commercial with a big, smiling, purple grape.

He reaches out and pats my hand. "You don't have to wash coffee cups, Carolyn."

"I really don't mind," I insist. "I just think the guys should do it, too. We should all wash the coffee cups. After all, we all use them."

Equality logic is lost on Jerry May, who may never have washed a cup in his life. "I understand," he says, his tone friendly, "but it's okay. I don't expect the art department to wash dishes." He apologizes for Jean, adding, "You shouldn't have been asked to do it."

That's the end of the subject of KP. However, I have succeeded in making a number-one enemy of Jean and alienating every other woman in the agency who naturally sides with her against the "bra-burning hippy girl from California."

* * *

I decide that the May Advertising logo, a busy, hopelessly dated design, should be redesigned in a more fresh, modern, simple, seventies look. Ed Felesky agrees with this idea, and I plunge ahead with new sketches.

I schedule a meeting and present a half-dozen concepts to Jerry. Today he wears an orange jumpsuit with the white patent accessories. He loves my new designs and selects two for further development.

A second round of tighter concepts, and he makes his final choice. Camera-ready art is prepared and the work order for new stationery, envelopes and business cards for everyone is given to the favorite Industrial Road printer of the moment.

During all this creative development, Bob Brown has been up in Lacey, Washington, tending to his Lacey newspaper.

Now he returns—and stops the presses.

He invites me into his office and closes the door. I know Bob likes me, so I figure I'm not in trouble, but I haven't a clue what's going on.

Bob is dead-set against updating the agency's print image.

"We're not doing new stationery," he says. "We're not changing anything."

In the manner of a parent to a child he explains to me that Jerry May started out as a camper salesman on Boulder Highway, and because of that he has kind of a flaky reputation.

"Our logo and stationery look this way to give the impression of old, banking-like, stability, to offset Jerry's reputation. And by the way, you guys have to stop burning incense in the art department. Jean is convinced somebody back there is smoking pot."

The printing purchase order is cancelled and all the work is thrown away. For a week, Jerry avoids my eye. I wonder how it is that among three partners, with only one active on a day-to-day basis, one partner can breeze in at the last minute and cancel out a decision made by another partner. I conclude that of the three, Bob must be the money guy, the one with the profitable business—the

*Valley Times*—who must have put up the money to open the agency in the first place.

Again, I choose to adapt rather than quit.

\* \* \*

Account executives at May Advertising are Doug James, David Canter, and fresh-out-of-University-of-Reno Sig Rogich, who in later years, as a reward for his Republican political work, will become the U.S. Ambassador to Iceland.

"Account executive" is a fancy name for salesman. The AE represents the agency to the client. If you can bring a big client— or several new clients—in the door, you can be an account executive.

Most of these AEs are under thirty. None of them know much about advertising and none know how to price and charge for design. My fancy L.A.-style job numbering and billing system has no effect. It is not that they don't understand it; I think they just choose to ignore it. Why bill the client just a few hundred dollars for a job if you can get a few thousand out of him?

I have no idea how client billing is calculated, but I know that for graphics it isn't on work done hourly, or any set price guideline.

When the University of Nevada Las Vegas, an account Sig brought in, screams about the cost of an alumni invitation, I show him the exact logged hours that the art department worked on it, including changes. He crosses out the amount billed, writes in a lower amount, writes his initials next to the new amount, and takes it back to accounting for re-billing. With this action, he will be a hero to his client.

Sig is not concerned that the agency lost money on this job. I don't think he even thinks about the accounting fact that when you pay an artist $15 an hour to do the work, and the artist works so many hours so that you end up billing the client $2 an hour for the job, you've lost money. I shake my head. By now, I've figured out that this loss on the UNLV job will be made up on an overcharge somewhere else, most likely to a hotel/casino client.

August nears its end, and *Panorama* says 50,000 visitors now descend monthly on Las Vegas.

At the end of the month, Jerry May, head-to-toe in lime green, comes into the art department accompanied by a young man carrying a black artist portfolio.

"I want you all to meet Greg," Jerry says. "He'll be joining us the week after next."

Now that he has a job, Greg will move from the mid-west to Las Vegas with his wife, Chadda. This job is important to him because Chadda, a hairdresser, won't be able to work until she satisfies Nevada's six-month resident waiting period for a cosmetology license.

Business must be good and the agency must be growing if we're adding another artist.

But two days later Jerry comes into the art department with another announcement: "We're rearranging the art department employee payroll system so that the agency will function better." He goes into a lengthy explanation of the new system that reminds me he used to be a camper salesman.

What this "rearrangement" means is that we artists will no longer be salaried employees; we will now be paid by the job. Jerry does not address the issue of how jobs will be handed out, and Ed is unclear as well. I envision all of us artists fighting over jobs as they come in.

Both Ed Felesky and the old guy who lays out the full-page car ads are exempt from this—they'll continue to get regular paychecks. The car ads are all the old guy does, it keeps him busy all day, and Jerry doesn't want to lose him or the auto dealership accounts. Ed, as his golf buddy, must of course be taken care of.

I can see that as the Art Director and also on salary, Ed will get to pick the jobs as they come in, and Jerry will pressure him to do as many of the jobs as possible in order to get his money's worth and not have to pay too much to the rest of us.

John and Billy and I now will be in effect free-lance artists, except that we won't make a real free-lancer's hourly income, and we will all be sitting around in one room waiting for work.

I see no future at May Advertising, and I admit I'm disappointed. I was kind of getting to like it there.

While Ed is out to his martini lunch, I ask the guys, "Do you think we should call Greg and tell him? I mean, they're moving out here thinking he's going to have this job."

John fiddles with a Rapidograph pen. "I dunno…"

Billy flips through a graphic arts magazine. "It's really none of our business."

So nobody calls Greg to tell him that by the time he and his wife arrive in Vegas, it's likely there will be no job for him.

That afternoon I make my decision. "I'm going home to sit by the pool," I tell Ed. "Call me if something comes in and you need me."

I have worked for May Advertising for almost three months, and I think they are all relieved to see me go. No more annoying hourly numbering system and now less competition for work hours.

A few months later, May Advertising goes under.

## CHAPTER 5 – Survival jobs

Joy Hammon leaves the Union Plaza and starts her own public relations firm. She hires me to do a few free-lance ads and brochures, but though it's a lot of fun to work with her, I don't make enough to live on.

Sig Rogich starts his own ad agency, R & R Advertising, with upscale offices on West Sahara. No office under the freeway for Sig. When I ask for a job, he tells me, "I can't afford you." I'm not sure what he means by that. But later when I do a $15. freelance job for him and wait nine months to be paid, I figure it meant he's cheap.

None of the other Las Vegas advertising agencies farm much work out, and no one is hiring. I decide Vegas is not a good city for a free-lance graphic designer. It looks as if the only women making any real money in this town are showgirls, cocktail waitresses, and hookers.

One morning while I'm scrambling eggs on the little stove in the trailer, Del says, "Our circus jobs aren't looking too likely."

"Yeah, bummer," I say.

Del pours himself a second cup of coffee. "I better go back to work. I'll call Neil."

"Good idea."

Del arranges for us to have breakfast with Neil, his former ATF boss. The three of us sit at Denny's on the Strip, working our way through eggs and pancakes and ham when Del and I get the big surprise.

While Del has been on his leave of absence, the Federal Bureau of Alcohol, Tobacco and Firearms has passed off its drug-chasing operations to the government's newly-formed Drug Enforcement Agency (DEA). Yes, Neil is the head of the new DEA office for the Southwest area, but no, he can't hire Del.

"You turned forty-six," Neil says.

Del slices off a hunk of ham. "What the hell does that have to do with anything?"

"Well, the new DEA has an age limit."

Remembering the media hype of the sixties and thinking about equal opportunity, I ask, "How can they have an age limit?"

Neil doesn't look at Del when he says, "It's forty-five."

This is a light-bulb moment for me, who would never have thought our government could have an age limit on jobs. "You mean, for the sake of a couple of months, even though he's on a leave of absence, he can't have his job back? It's a leave of absence—isn't he technically still a government employee?"

"I'd hire you back in a hot minute," Neil says to Del. "I don't have anybody as qualified or experienced as you, but my hands are tied. It's the law."

As a child of the sixties, I am incensed. I seem to recall something called the Age Discrimination in Employment Act of 1967 protecting people who are forty years of age or older.

"You're practicing age discrimination!" I rage.

"I suppose," Neil says. "But I can't fix it." He signals the waitress for more coffee.

Del says, "What a crock of shit."

The waitress pours our coffee, but I don't wait for her to leave the table to express myself. "They can't do that! There's a law against age discrimination! We'll sue the federal government!"

Neil looks startled.

Del turns pale. "No, honey, we aren't going to sue the federal government."

"Why not? Tell me just why not?" I envision headlines in the *L.A. Times*. I envision Washington paying Del a big hunk of settlement money.

Neil sips his coffee without comment. His face shows no reaction when Del says, "Because they don't play fair, and I don't want them poking around any more into my background."

That stops me. Del had told me he originally selected to work for ATF over the CIA because "the CIA is ruthless. If they decide you're dispensable while you're in the field, they pull out your support, only they don't tell you. If the bad guys don't get you, you're always at risk that your own government will."

I can't believe this. Here is a guy with an incredible record of government service. Just a few months over this new DEA age limit and our government is going to throw away this experienced employee.

In the car, I fume all the way back to the trailer. This is so unfair and I still want to sue the bastards.

"Really. I don't want those guys digging around," Del repeats. "You can never tell what they'll come up with to use against you."

"Like what?"

"Like things that are better left dead."

"Dead?"

"In the past."

"Things you did?"

Del's lips spread in a sly smile. "Things I don't want to answer questions about."

So, I wonder, does this mean that maybe he's actually killed people?

We ride a few more blocks in silence while I consider this. In the past he's been free with the stories he's told me, but I get that now he doesn't want to go into detail.

Knowing Del's independent nature, I suppose that there were plenty of times in the "line of duty" when he stretched the rules of the game, even stretched the boundaries of the law. I don't want to believe the man I love has killed people, because I don't want that to affect how I feel about him, but....

In any case Del is adamant. There will be no age discrimination lawsuit against the U.S. government. We will keep our mouths shut, if we know what's good for us. I get the picture as it relates to me. I don't ask any more questions.

I still don't think it's fair, but it is his job. If he doesn't want to pursue it, there is nothing I can do. Guess I will go back to sunning myself by the pool, a nice environment in which to contemplate what I'm going to do next for income.

Later that same day Neil calls Del on the phone. He sympathizes with our situation and wants to help. "I know a guy who might need security," he says. "Jack Binion, down at the Horseshoe. Go talk to him. Tell him I sent you."

\* \* \*

When we first arrived in Vegas, Del took me to the downtown Fremont Street hotel/casino, Binion's Horseshoe, to see their famous glass-encased exhibit of a million dollars in real money. The basement oyster bar and the coffee shop with real waffles—it's said the owner eats them every morning—have already made the place one of our favorites.

The Horseshoe is also known as the first Las Vegas hotel with an elevator and air conditioning. Emphasizing personalized customer service, quality food, extra-high betting limits and hand's-on management, gaming legend Lester "Benny" Binion has built quite a successful and profitable gaming operation.

Jack Binion, Benny's oldest son, hires Del to be a security guard. During the following weeks, Del comes home from his day shift in the casino with amazing tales, which he shares with me and Neil and Bill.

One day Security catches a female purse-snatcher, but lets her go. She is ninety years old and it would be bad publicity to have her arrested. Another day a man comes raging into the casino brandishing a meat cleaver. The police are called, but nobody comes. Del disarms the man, takes the meat cleaver over to the police department and slams it into the wooden desk of the sergeant on duty.

"That got their attention," he says. Neil and Bill laugh out loud. My Del is a real man's man.

I ask, "What about that rumor I heard that Benny has guys in the back alley drive a car over the hands of any dealer caught stealing?" Del either knows nothing about it, or isn't talking.

He makes fun of Jack's younger brother, Teddy Binion: "He's a real dopehead." Del isn't sure if Jack knows Teddy smokes weed, but says, "It's pretty obvious Teddy's stoned all the time." Del isn't about to say anything to Jack. This is Binion family stuff. "None of my business," he says.

* * *

Now that Del's working, I need to get busy, too.

Desert Décor, the only art store in town, is moving to a larger location up the street on East Charleston Boulevard. I met Bob, the owner, when I was working for Jerry May. Since I am not working, I ask if they need any help moving, and Bob hires me for three days. It is still summer in Vegas and I really earn my money carrying boxes in the heat. I hope I might find a lead through this activity to another graphics job, but nothing comes of it.

I'm reduced to reading the newspapers, scanning the want-ads for anything I think I can do.

One ad in the *Las Vegas Sun* seems promising. Vic Havas Motors, a camper dealership at 3800 Boulder Highway, seeks a secretary. The pay is attractive, more than listed in any other secretarial ad. I call the business and schedule an appointment for an interview.

At the dealership I meet with the owner himself, Vic Havas. Casually dressed in flared slacks, his wide-collared shirt is unbuttoned two-thirds of the way down his chest, revealing the gold chains. His sideburns are neatly trimmed. Everything about him reeks high-pressure salesman. He leads me to his upstairs office, where a long, slanted glass window overlooks the showroom.

I present my resumé. He's reading it and nodding. "I can handle advertising as well," I tell him. "I have a portfolio of ads I've done. Would you like to see it?"

Yes he would, but not at his desk. He guides me to a black leather couch on the other side of the office, where we sit side by side to look at my portfolio. I have it open on the glass coffee table when he begins to talk about "other work."

I'm so surprised by this turn in the conversation that it takes me a minute to figure out what he means. Then he puts his hand on my knee and tells me I will have to have sex with him, which of course he is willing to pay for.

Surely he's joking. So I make a joke, too. Shifting my knee away from his hand, I say, "If I were going to do that, it would cost a whole lot more than the salary of a secretarial job."

Havas gives me an angry smirk. "Why should I pay you hundreds of dollars when every showgirl in town is giving it away for twenty-five bucks?"

He's not joking. I realize that I am alone with this man in this office, and I have no idea how far he will go. I need to keep my cool and get out of here fast. I don't want a scene, but I'm ready to scream long and loud.

I close my portfolio, stand up so that I can step away from him, and say, "If every showgirl in town is doing it for twenty-five dollars, you don't need me."

On unsteady legs I march out, slam the door behind me, and don't look back. So much for the "secretarial interview."

Del is home when I return to The Lone Palm.

"You won't believe what I just went through," I say. I tell him what happened, how I can't believe the nerve of this Vic Havas guy.

To my astonishment, Del laughs.

"Lorraine had the same experience," he says. Lorraine is Del's former girl friend, the sister of Judi's boyfriend. Lorraine lived with Del in Las Vegas years earlier when he owned his Continental Property Management Company. "I remember it now. Must be the same guy. She was really pissed."

"I don't blame her," I say. "I'm pissed, too. What a jerk!"

Del repeats my story to Bill and Neil.

That evening he tells me, "Bill says Vic Havas only runs that ad in the newspaper to get girls to come to his office so he can rape them."

Unbelievable.

Eventually karma takes care of Vic Havas. Del figures he finally hit on a girl with a mob-connected husband or boyfriend or father. In any case, someone was beyond angry. Havas is found dead in the desert outside of Las Vegas—naked, stabbed, garroted, burned and castrated.

* * *

The idea of being a showgirl always intrigued me. I loved the 1970 film *The Grasshopper*, with Jacqueline Bisset. I loved its glitzy portrayal of Vegas life and glossed right over its more depressing life messages.

In 1965 when I was a Playboy Bunny in Detroit, one night on television I saw the International Showgirl Competition. They asked the showgirl who won what her biggest dream in life was, and she answered, "To be a Playboy Bunny." I thought that was so funny, since I was a Bunny dreaming about being a showgirl.

The two best-known production shows in Vegas are Don Arden's *Lido De Paris* at the Stardust and the *Folies Bergere* at the Tropicana. The *Lido* is the longest running, having opened in 1958 at the same time as the Stardust itself. Not to be outdone by another hotel, the following year Tropicana entertainment director Lou Walters—Barbara Walters' father—brought the *Folies* from Paris.

So one afternoon I go to the Stardust and find my way backstage. It is cavernous and dark, with lots of hanging props and ropes and rigging. A whole lot bigger than the backstage of my high school theater. Voices and other sounds echo.

I ask around and am directed to the tiny office of the guy in charge of hiring showgirls. Papers and costumes are stacked everywhere. I introduce myself. He moves some feathery headdresses from a chair so I can sit down.

He is impressed that I was a Playboy Bunny. "How tall are you?" he asks.

"Five, ten."

We chat, and then comes the moment of truth: he asks me to stand up and take off my shirt and bra so he can evaluate my breasts.

I have given a lot of thought to how I'll feel about this. I tested for Playmate of the month, so I have taken off my clothes for a photographer, and the idea of showing my breasts to a crowded theater doesn't bother me.

But now I'm nervous. Is it because I'm auditioning for a job? Because it's warm in the room? Or because this guy is staring right at my breasts, judging them?

It becomes a moot point when he tells me, yes, I qualify to appear in the Lido, but right now they are not hiring. No, he doesn't know when there will be an opening.

Next stop, the Trop. Same routine. This time I'm not nervous. Yes, I qualify.

"We have an opening for a swing girl," the guy tells me.

This is an entry-level job. The Swing Girl replaces showgirls who are sick or who go on vacation. I imagine it's a hard job because you'd have to know virtually everybody's position in the show, like memorizing every character's lines in a play.

Now I learn the truth about the money. Being a showgirl means you work two shows a night, six nights a week. The "dark night"—always a weekday—is your only day off. The only weeks the show is dark are the first two weeks in December.

The swing girl job pays $200 a week. This is less than Jerry May was paying me, and I must supply and pay for my own dance shoes, fishnet stockings, eyelashes, and all that makeup.

I think about being a cocktail waitress again and do the math. Most likely, I can make more money as a cocktail waitress, and have two days a week off. I also don't have to worry about sunning myself and getting a tan line—unlike Playboy Bunnies, showgirls are not allowed to have tan lines.

As much as I am attracted to feathers and glitz and rhinestones and lights, practicality wins out over show biz. I turn down the swing girl job in the *Folies Bergere*.

\* \* \*

It is September. The crawling summer shows no sign of ending any time soon. I am hot and bored and desperate for a job, desperate to make enough money to go back to Los Angeles. Del and I have not discussed leaving Las Vegas, but it's a small town, and neither one of us is doing too well in the career department.

Right after turning down the *Folies Bergere*, I answer another newspaper ad, this time for a bikini dancer at the Troubadour, a nightclub on Western Avenue in the same neighborhood as the now-defunct May Advertising.

How hard can go-go dancing be? Judy did it in L.A. and made good money. And it isn't the kind of job for which you have to feel any loyalty. I can quit as soon as I save enough money to leave town; I have not lost sight of my number one goal.

At the afternoon "audition" they play a disco record and, in shorts and halter top and to the best of my ability, I gyrate my hips. The club owner, Frank Canul, and two other guys—one I think is the bartender—watch.

They don't appear to be impressed with my dancing skills. Frank Canul, kind of a creepy guy with hunched shoulders, says, "We don't have an opening here right now."

I think, then why the ad in the newspaper? Are they pulling a Vic Havas?

Then Canul says, "Too bad you don't know cocktails."

"But I do know cocktails," I say. "I know all the drinks. I was a Playboy Bunny."

"Great. We need a girl for a lunch shift." He writes down an address and telephone number on a slip of paper and hands it to me. "Take this over to the Jungle Club and tell them I sent you." Besides owning part of the Troubadour, Frank Canul is a partner in this little Paradise Road Mexican restaurant called the Jungle Club.

I drive east down Flamingo and turn onto Paradise Road, following the directions on the paper. I fantasize about a lucrative cocktail job that will let me accumulate a lot of money in a short time and try not to get my hopes up.

While thinking about this, I miss the left turn at Paradise. Next thing I know I am at Maryland Parkway, where Flamingo narrows abruptly to two lanes. I've gone too far. I go through the light, make a U-ey at the first opportunity and head back west on Flamingo Road.

I find The Jungle Club, a small, free-standing building set back by itself from Paradise Road on a little street called Naples Avenue.

Inside the restaurant it is so dark I can't see anything until my eyes adjust from the afternoon sunlight. I can barely make out a dining room with booths and a separate cocktail lounge. The Jungle Club is typical of 70s restaurants and bars in the desert. No windows to let in heat or light so you'd know it's time to go home because the sun is coming up.

Frank Canul's partner hires me. I begin working Monday through Friday from 11 a.m. to 3 p.m. serving cocktails. There are no office buildings nearby, and the lunch crowd is mostly men in some phase of the construction business. A lot of them own various construction and building material businesses and are friends of Frank Canul. They like me and tip really well.

Right now there is a lot of building going on in Las Vegas. One of my customers, a man who owns a structural steel company, tells me, "It can't go on much longer. We're running out of water. This valley will never support 200,000 people." By that time, I think to myself, I plan to be out of here.

I get the impression these guys want to build fast, make a bunch of money, and get out before "the end" comes. After that, they don't care what happens to Las Vegas. It makes me think of old western mining towns, of which there are many in Nevada, that dried up into abandoned ghost towns after the mines played out.

At the end of my second week working at the Jungle Club I am making as much in tips as I was as "associate art director" at May Advertising—and working half the hours. I am also making more than I would have as the *Folies Bergere* swing showgirl.

One day the bartender, Erven, presses me to go in with him on a system to steal. Erven is an old guy in his fifties, as tall as I am, with a beer belly and a perpetual sneer.

"Let me put it this way," he whispers. "If you don't cooperate, you won't be working here very long."

I have experienced this kind of situation before, serving drinks at both a Hilton and a Sheraton in Los Angeles while I was getting my Commercial Art degree. This stealing in bars is not all that unusual. One thing I always appreciated about the Playboy Club—there was never any pressure to do anything other than the job you were hired to do. In fact, they liked to hire girls who had never been cocktail waitresses before, specifically because those girls wouldn't bring bad habits into the Club, like stealing.

I like and need this job at the Jungle Club, and I don't want to create a bad working environment, so I agree to "work with" Erven.

Before my eyes, Erven turns right into a greedy pig. My motto in this kind of situation is conservative: take a little, leave a little. I have seen overly-ambitious cocktail waitresses get fired from lucrative jobs, and vowed that would never happen to me. After padding one customer's running tab with another couple's drinks, I tell Erven, "Enough. No more for today."

I want to get enough money to get out of here and back to L.A., and if I am going to steal to accomplish it, I want to steal on my terms.

Erven becomes hostile, but there isn't much he can do since I control the table drink checks, thus collecting for all the drinks that he doesn't serve directly to customers at the bar. We continue to work together under an uneasy truce.

* * *

Each day before my lunch shift I have to punch a time card at a time clock inside the back door and walk through the kitchen into the restaurant. The kitchen at the Jungle Club is full of Mexican workers who speak no English, and they like me.

"*Buenos dias, Carolina! Como esta usted?*" the guys yell.

I don't speak Spanish and don't know how to reply.

Juan, a pretty young boy with a disarming smile who knows a little English says, "You say, '*muy bueno.*'"

Okay.

Next morning: "*Como esta usted, Carolina?*"

My best smile. "*Muy bueno.*"

The kitchen erupts with laughter. They *really* like me. What a great way to start work.

This daily scenario becomes one of my fondest memories of the Jungle Club.

One day a few months after I quit to go to work at the MGM Grand, Del tells me his singer friend Dick Hale is opening at the Las Vegan Club, a place on Flamingo opposite the MGM. Dick wants to take us to an early dinner, before his 9 p.m. show. Since Dick's wife is from Mexico City, Del and I take them to the Jungle Club.

Juan, who brings the water, chips and guacamole, recognizes me. "*Carolina! Como esta usted?*"

"*Muy bueno, gracias.*"

He chuckles all the way back to the kitchen.

Dick's Mexican wife gives me a strange look. "Do you know what you just said?" she asks.

"I said, 'I'm fine, thank you.'"

"Not exactly," she says, giggling. "You should say, '*muy bien.*' What you said means, 'I'm hot stuff', as in really good, you know, in bed."

When we're presented with menus, the waiter recognizes me and asks, "*Como esta usted, Carolina?*" I give him the correct response, "*Muy bien*", along with a sarcastic look.

He laughs and says, "Ah, somebody told you."

## CHAPTER 6 – The Las Vegas International Circus

A space becomes available in the permanent mobile home section of the Lone Palm. Del arranges to move the Wilderness there. We are thrilled to have shade from the trees and a little yard.

Our new neighbors are Olga, the Peruvian change girl at Circus Circus, and a retired couple who used to be in a country western band in the '50's. He was injured in an industrial accident, and she takes in sewing.

To give our new elm-shaded patio some privacy, Del builds a six-foot redwood fence on the side facing the lane. We buy a redwood picnic table and some outdoor potted plants. I plant seeds for sweet pea flowers, which I've loved since my mother grew them in our backyard in Seattle. It doesn't go well; apparently sweet peas don't like a desert climate. Who would think there would be such a thing as too much sun?

Though I know I'll never be able to call this town "home", Del and I begin to have a settled life in Las Vegas. Our jobs are going well and I'm actually saving money. With every day that passes, my obsession with moving back as soon as possible to Los Angeles lessens. I'll leave Las Vegas eventually, but now there doesn't seem to be a big hurry.

We're still in contact with the Farfans, but going on the road with the Las Vegas International Circus no longer holds its previous adventurous appeal.

However visiting the Pearl house is like going on a holiday. One afternoon we're invited to stay for dinner. There must be twenty people around the big dining room table. Plenty of food and conversation and laughter. As head of the family, Carlos sits at the head of the table.

One of the young aerial ballet performers has a three-month-old baby. He is passed around the table like the main *pollo* dish, so that everyone can hold him and cuddle and coo over him.

When he's handed to Carlos, the catcher positions his huge palm into a chair seat around the baby's bum, and holds him upright. Carlos raises his hand high over his head and waves the seated baby back and forth.

I'm mesmerized, terrified the baby will fall. Around me I hear cheers of delight. No one but me seems at all concerned for the child's safety.

Someone calls, "Bravo, *bebe!*"

Baby gurgles and laughs. He loves this. Does he think this is a normal childhood game?

Theresa laughs at my shock. "This is how our children learn not to be afraid of heights," she says. "Someday the boy will be a great trapeze artist."

I remember the child-size trapeze in the backyard. Theresa says, "All the children play on it as soon as they can walk and climb."

One day Del and I arrive at the Pearl house to find it suspiciously quiet. No one comes out to greet us. We knock on the front door, which is usually unlocked. No answer.

"Let's go 'round back," Del says. We walk around the side of the house and begin to hear small voices in the backyard. Four little boys look up at us as we come into their view. There is not an adult in sight.

"Hi," Del says. "Where is everybody?"

Five-year-old Tato says, "Gino fell off the trapeze and cracked his head. They all gone to the hospital."

Gino is Armando and Anna's ten-year-old son. The younger Tato is Armando Farfan, Jr.

Just then we hear noise at the street. The boys follow us back to the front of the house, where Gino, helped by his mother, climbs out of a car. Several other adults and children get out of other cars.

Tato and the other boys run to Gino, who has an impressive white bandage wrapped around his head. He's proud to show it off.

"He's fine," Theresa says. "Just a concussion."

\* \* \*

In November Carlos finally takes his circus on the road, down to Central America. How I would have loved to go! What an adventure it could have been. Part of me is angry at him for not getting his act together sooner.

But Del and I have jobs now, and Carlos says he doesn't have the money to pay us. "Maybe next season," he says.

It would be several months before we hear anything more about the Las Vegas International Circus. One day at the supermarket Del and I run into Janet, one of the American aerial ballet girls.

"Is the circus back?" I ask.

Janet shudders. "Jeez, we barely got out with our lives," she says.

"What happened?"

"Carlos has been arrested," she says. "He is in El Salvador."

This turns out to be one adventure I count myself lucky to have missed.

Janet says beefy, tanned, macho Carlos, accustomed to being in charge, pissed off the wrong *policia*. Everyone was thrown into jail.

"It was horrible. For days we weren't given any food at all."

I notice that Janet has lost a lot of weight. She's a small girl anyway, but now her forearms are the size of my wrist. She looks lost in her baggy tee shirt and her blond hair doesn't look healthy. She's been back in town for three days, and her grocery cart is stacked, as if she thinks she'll never have a chance to buy food again.

She continues, telling us, "All the circus rigging and equipment were confiscated. Even Anna's poodles."

"And the Farfans?" Del asks.

Janet stares at a spot way beyond the end of the grocery aisle. "I don't know."

The Las Vegas International Circus is effectively disbanded. Eventually, everyone is deported from El Salvador to their country of origin according to their passports. Janet is the first of the American girls who formed the aerial ballet to arrive back in Las Vegas.

It would be two years before the Farfan family and the last of the troop make their way back into town.

## CHAPTER 7 – Blue-eyed blondes

All summer the Las Vegas newspapers have run stories about the new MGM Grand Hotel, scheduled to open December 1.

This will be the first mega hotel to open on the Strip since Caesars Palace in 1966. The newspapers are calling Kirk Kerkorian, the owner/designer, "The Avis of Las Vegas." Howard Hughes, with his impressive fortune, has bought six hotels, I guess making him the Hertz of Las Vegas. Kerkorian's worth in comparison is only $274 million.

"*Variety* is calling Kirk Kerkorian, the biggest closet millionaire since Howard Hughes," Del says. I didn't even know Del had ever read *Variety*. "He's the design ego behind this thing that they say will be the world's largest gambling resort."

We're having our morning coffee with Bill in the Lone Palm office. Outside, the sun blazes, the temperature already in the high nineties, and it isn't even 9 a.m.

"Twenty-four million to build Caesars," Bill says.

Del explains to me that Caesars was the first theme casino/hotel with a layout designed so that visitors must walk through the casino in order to reach the restaurants, showrooms, shops and swimming pool. For seven years Caesars has held sway as the largest, grandest hotel on the famous Las Vegas Strip. "Oh, other hotels opened with about a hundred rooms, like the Bonanza in '67, but none of 'em challenged Caesars' exalted position," Del says."

Joanne has appeared with the fresh pot of coffee and has heard this last part of the conversation. "Until the MGM Grand," she says. "Where are they going to build it again?"

Bill holds out his cup so she can pour him fresh coffee. "Southeast corner of Flamingo and the Strip. Right kitty-corner from Caesars. They're gonna tear down the Bonanza."

"So who's this Kirk Kerkorian?" I ask. I'd never heard of him before coming to Las Vegas. "And how did he get to be so rich?"

Del and Bill know all about the man. They are happy to educate me. "In the 'fifties," Bill says, "he owned an air service, flew Hollywood celebrities at a hundred bucks a head to Vegas for quickie weddings and divorces. Then the Last Frontier contracted him to fly high rollers and celebrities back and forth."

Del adds, "He bought that land on the northwest corner of Flamingo and the Strip in the early 'sixties for less than a million. What a deal! Thirty-four acres for less than a million! Then he sold it to Jay Sarno for five million so Sarno could build Caesars Palace."

I learn that Kerkorian sold his Los Angeles charter service and in 1967 purchased the failing Flamingo Hotel. The following year he bought the Bonanza Hotel & Casino, across the street from The Dunes. By the early seventies he also owned controlling interests in Western Airlines and Hollywood's Metro-Goldwyn-Mayer (MGM) studios.

Kerkorian's first casino dream was the thirty-story International, which opened in 1969 on land off Paradise Road. "Bought that land for five million and spent sixty building it," Bill says.

Del asks, "Got any more coffee?"

Bill looks at the now empty glass pot on the single burner hotplate next to the cash register. "Joanne!" he yells, "We're out of coffee!"

Joanne yells back from the kitchen behind the office. "Okay, I'll make more!" God forbid, Bill should go back and make a pot himself.

The coffee subject handled, Del says, "Caesars has 700 rooms, the International about 1,500. Even being next to the Convention Center, it hasn't been much competition for Caesars. But that MGM—2,100 rooms!" Like Bill, Del likes to talk numbers.

"Who do they think will fill them?" Bill scoffs. "They're gonna have a tough time keeping their occupancy rate up."

"What's 'occupancy rate'?" I ask.

"That's the percentage of people who are booked into rooms every day." Del says.

Bill glances to the door leading to the kitchen, expecting Joanne to bring the new pot of coffee any minute. "That Kerkorian had the personal touch," he says. "At the International, you could mingle with celebrities and the owner."

Del says, "Hughes kept himself secluded, and he still filled his casino."

"Yeah, but Kerkorian walked around talking to everybody and handing out comps for food and drinks and shows. The stars who worked the showroom gambled in the casino, and he made sure they were easy for fans to approach."

"And you think all that personality created a loyal following? I don't see how they can do anything like that in a casino the size of this new MGM."

Now that Kerkorian's dreaming of a resort themed after the MGM Studios, he's created a hot buzz in town. The Flamingo and the International have been sold to the Hilton Hotels Corporation, and Kerkorian has purchased the forty-three acres of Strip property surrounding the Bonanza.

Right after Del and I arrived in Las Vegas in April, we began to hear talk about this huge new hotel due to open in December. At the time, I didn't pay much attention. December was a long way off and I'd figured by then we'd be on the road with the circus.

In August, MGM personnel director Bill Champion announces they will be "accepting applications Monday through Saturday, from 10 a.m. to 3 p.m. in the East Hall of the Las Vegas Convention Center."

Applying for work at the MGM is now the major entertainment event in town. Everyone goes to fill out an application. It's the thing to do. Friends go in groups, with an outing afterwards to lunch at the Coachmen's Inn, the Village Pub, or the Alpine Village to discuss their chances of being hired.

With no Las Vegas girlfriends, but plenty of encouragement from the men around me, one day I trot off to the Convention Center to fill out an application.

I wear pressed slacks, a sleeveless blouse, a business-looking jacket, minimal make-up and jewelry, and sensible shoes. A very California job-application outfit. As soon as I'm inside the Convention Center, I feel like I must really stand out among all these people in tank tops and tee shirts and shorts and jeans.

The forms are scattered on the fold-up tables. A cacophony of conversation, scraping chairs, and friends greeting friends fills the cavernous hall. I pick up an application form, sit down at the end of one of the tables and pull a pen from my purse. I'm dreaming again: wouldn't it be way cool to work as a graphic designer in the art department of a big, new Vegas hotel…?

At the bottom of the form where you list previous employment is a line labeled, "Other." I scribble, "Playboy Bunny cocktail waitress." Not relevant to my grand career as a graphic designer, but at least I wrote something to complete my employment history.

I'd heard a rumor that the MGM isn't going to hire any women over twenty-six. It sounds absurd, but I figure this town's so crazy, it just might be true. So I lie about my age on my application. Who can tell twenty-six from twenty-nine?

My attention is drawn by noisy activity at the other end of the table. Three girls and a guy pull out chairs, scraping metal across cement, and sit. Each grabs an application form. The girls rummage in their big purses for pens. They begin to write, and to compare notes.

One girl with scraggly hair, wearing a tie-dyed shirt over a peasant skirt, asks her friend, "Who are you putting down for a reference?"

The guy, in his early twenties, is good-looking in an outdoorsy way. Except he's wearing a pink, pointy-collared shirt open far enough down his hairless chest to show off three heavy-linked gold chains. He lights a cigarette and says, "Oh, don't worry about it."

The other girl frowns and fusses with a lock of her strawberry blond hair. She's completely dressed in white. She's even pulled from her purse a white ballpoint pen. "If you don't know somebody high up, it won't make any difference anyway," she murmurs.

"So do you know anybody?"

"No. Do you?"

They all stop writing and look at each other.

"You know, if you don't have any juice, you probably won't get hired," Scraggly says.

The girl in white chews on the end of her white pen. "I did hear you have to know somebody to get hired at the MGM."

The guy blows cigarette smoke out of the side of his mouth. "Yeah, I heard that, too."

"So if we don't have any juice..." Scraggly pauses and lays her pen across her app. "This is really going to be a long shot," she says.

The guy's cigarette smoke blowing turns into a sigh. "Yeah, probably."

"So why bother?"

They all look at each other, as if critical thinking has just occurred.

"This is probably a waste of time," the blond pen-chewer in white says.

Scraggly nods. "Yeah, they're not going to hire us without any juice."

The guy chain-lights another cigarette. "Let's get out of here."

Scraggly shoves back her chair, a screeching noise, and picks up her purse. "You're right. This is a waste of time."

And they're gone, leaving half-filled-out applications on the table. Talked themselves right out of applying for a job at the newest hotel in town.

I don't have any juice, either, but it doesn't matter because with any luck I won't be here by the time December rolls around, anyway. Four months is a long time—anything could happen. I have no intention of staying in Las Vegas. Surely in four months I can make enough money to get back to the real world, back to L.A.

Nevertheless, I get in line to hand my application to the stocky Italian man with long black sideburns who sits behind a makeshift desk. When my turn comes, he reads quickly down the page—does he even know what a graphic designer is?—and looks up at me. His smile is broad and approving, his teeth fat and perfect.

"I see here you have experience as a cocktail waitress."

"Yes, but I'm applying for the Graphic Arts department."

He shakes his head. "You don't want that job. You won't make any money. Besides, those jobs are already filled by friends of the owners. I'm going to put you down as a cocktail waitress. You'll make a lot of money. I'm going to give you an A-rating." Big toothy smile, leveled at my boobs. "You'll be great."

I lose interest in changing his mind. "Whatever."

* * *

September progresses. Every day in the dark Jungle Club one of my male customers asks, "Have you applied to the MGM?"

I don't want word to get back to Frank Canul that I might be planning to leave, so I laugh and say, "Hasn't everybody?"

Late one afternoon in early October I'm sitting at home in the trailer, hiding from the heat—when does it end?—and the phone rings.

Del answers, "Hello?"

A gravelly male voice demands, "Carolyn there?"

My man bristles at the tone of this other man's voice. "Yeah. Who wants to know?"

"Tell her it's Danny Litwack from the MGM."

Without another word, Del hands me the phone.

Mr. Litwack, the Food and Beverage Manager, and a no-nonsense guy, tells me I'm invited to come in for a personal interview with the management. He gives me the day, the time, the place. His last businesslike words before he hangs up are, "Wear high heels, short shorts and smile like Hell."

On the appointed day, I arrive at the MGM Grand's temporary executive offices—in a former motel off Harmon Avenue, now surrounded by chain-link fencing and construction activity. I park the yellow mustang in the dirt.

As I get out of the car, a strong wind grabs at my hair. Balls of dust swirl up from the ground. In my shorts and highest heels I wobble to the door with care, peeking through my fingers that cover my eyes to protect my contact lenses.

By now, rumors are tossing like tumbleweeds all over town about "what they're looking for." Del told me, "The best cocktail waitress jobs are in the pit. That's where you want to be, in the pit." He's talking about the area of the casino where the dice, baccarat and blackjack tables are located.

In the crowded waiting area of these makeshift executive offices, I can hear the eerie sound of the wind outside forcing its way through the flimsy walls of this old motel. I notice a layer of fine sand on the top of the nearest desk.

The girl who sits next to me says to the girl on her other side, "They're only going to hire blue-eyed blondes to work the pit." She happens to be a blue-eyed blonde and the other girl, who like me is brunette, looks startled.

Okay, if this rumor is true, that leaves me out of the pit. So where will I end up? I don't even know what other cocktail jobs there are in a casino.

The standard rumor is still that if you aren't sleeping with a big boss or somebody who knows somebody, you won't get hired. I figure that can't be entirely true because when I was job-hunting before I found the Jungle Club the lady bar manager at the Union Plaza told me, "Don't you let anybody tell you that you have to sleep with somebody to get a job in these hotels. These guys can't sleep with everybody, it's just not physically possible."

Now I remember that I lied about my age on my application. I hope today they don't ask for ID. I haven't thought that far ahead and I have no idea what I should say.

From the conversation among the other applicants I learn that the MGM will be a union hotel, so the initial hiring is the only opportunity the bosses have to select any pretty girl they like. You don't have to be a member of the culinary union. The first 30 days will be a trial period, during which anyone can be fired at will. After that, you have the union behind you, and they can only fire you with documented reason, after a series of warning slips.

Finally my name is called and I'm shown into a tiny room where I meet Danny Litwack in person. He has my application on the desk in front of him. He doesn't ask me to sit down, so I strike a kind of modeling pose, arranging one leg in front of the other, knees slightly bent. I remember to "smile like hell." Litwack looks me up and down, then asks me a couple of questions that are already answered on my application.

Wonder of wonders, older than twenty-six and with no juice whatsoever, they hire me—but after all, I *am* a former Playboy Bunny.

\* \* \*

November 14, 1973 I go into the office of Jungle Club owner/manager Frank Canul to give my official notice. He's seated behind his desk, smoking a cigarette. The air is stale, so I don't close the door. I can still hear the Rolling Stones' *Angie* wailing from the jukebox by the front door of the restaurant.

Frank looks up from his paperwork. "Yeah?"

In spite of the bad air, I find myself taking a big breath to fortify my courage. In truth I have nothing to be nervous about, but I feel uncomfortable anyway.

"Well, what is it?" Frank snaps.

"I'm quitting at the end of the month. I've been hired at the MGM."

Even though Frank Canul knows tips from a lunch shift at the Jungle Club can't compete with the lure of big money to be made in a gigantic casino, he gives a disgusted snort and says, "You're making a big mistake."

He goes on in a rant to warn me about what I already know—the thirty-day trial before union "protection" kicks in. Then he eyes my body up and down, makes an obscene gesture with his cigarette, and says, "You know, honey, you won't be there after the first thirty days if you don't give great head."

His attitude has angered me. I am disgusted. Before I flounce out of his office, I lean forward to display more cleavage, look Frank Canul straight in the eye, and whisper, "Well, I guess I don't have anything to worry about then because as a matter of fact, I do."

* * *

Next step is the uniform fitting. By now hotel construction is completed enough that the cocktail waitresses can meet in the new dressing room. Wooden benches front rows of lockers. Overhead lights are bright and there are no windows. At the back of the room is a desk.

We are introduced to Evelyn, a short woman of ample proportion and dyed black hair who we are told will be the equivalent of the Bunny Mother. Real Bunny Mothers have a lot of responsibility—hiring, scheduling shifts, firing, and providing grooming tips and personal counseling—and I soon figure out that Evelyn's only job is to see that costumes are properly fitted and maintained.

Visionary Kerkorian selected the MGM Grand Hotel name based on the old Garbo film, *Grand Hotel*. Given that theme, the cocktail waitress costume design is a sexy adaptation of the movie's bellboy uniform. We will wear a short, flared skirt and strapless bustier made of red velour. Red Danskin panties over black pantyhose. Red velour velcroed collar and cuffs, and a pillbox "bellboy" hat, all trimmed in black braid and gold buttons.

Bra cups are larger than your real size and are expected to be stuffed. A real Bunny Mother would show you the best way to do that. Evelyn hasn't a clue. The bustiers are so short-waisted that tall girls like me have to walk with shoulders forward in order to keep boobs and pads in place. I soon discover that if I stand up straight and make any sudden movement, everything could pop out.

"Why can't this thing fit?" I complain, tugging at the top of my bustier.

Evelyn hesitates, and in a low voice says, "I think the dresses are short-waisted because the San Diego costume company they hired is having them made in Mexico."

Next the bosses will give a final look-see, supposedly to decide which girl will be assigned to which shift and station.

"This is stupid," the red-haired girl standing next to me says. "They pretty much already know who will be working where. They just want to be the first to ogle us in our new uniforms."

Now all costumed in red, we line up in the hallway. Girls who know each other group together. There are lots of sneaky and not-so-sneaky glances at each other, appraising make-up, hair styles, breast sizes. I notice quite a range of body shapes and heights and sizes—no one particular "look."

This makes me think of the subjectivity of Playboy's famous "bunny image." Technically explained as "the-girl-next-door look", it usually ends up being subject to the interpretation of each individual club manager. Keith Hefner, Hugh's brother, runs club operations, and one time he had a new blond girl friend who looked terrific in tangerine red lipstick. The word came down to all the clubs that the Bunnies were required to wear this particular shade of lipstick. My best red has a lot of blue in it, and I looked wiped out and stupid in tangerine. That insanity ended when Keith broke up with the girl. So much for "the Bunny image." As writer William Zinsser says, "One man's romantic sunrise is another man's hangover."

Now we're led into the employees' cafeteria—in the Vegas hotel business it's called the Help's Hall—where we can sit and wait to be called. Of 133 cocktail waitresses, five are black. They sit together at one table. I don't know if this is because they know each other or because they feel more comfortable together.

The girls at my table stare at them. One says, "Gee, in these hats they look like little organ grinder monkeys."

I can't believe what I'm hearing. How can she say that? The world is supposed to be past that kind of remark. Doesn't she know this is the seventies? Well, maybe only in California.

Me in the MGM cocktail waitress costume

The boss/judges consist of MGM president Al Benedict, executive vice-president Bernie Rothkopf, food and beverage manager Danny Litwack, bar manager Lenny Agnello and his assistant, Milton Scafika. With pens and notepads, they sit at a long table. At the end of the table, to one side, stands Morrie Jaeger, the casino manager, also there to check out these women who will become known as "MGM girls." Cinched and stuffed, we will parade one by one in front of them.

As a Playboy Bunny, I wore a ribbon rosette pinned to my hip with a centerpiece of plastic on which was engraved my name. The MGM must think they are saving money by only making little red circle pins with black numbers on them—no names to throw away if a girl leaves. These pins we wear on the top edge of the bustier. I am number forty-six.

My number is called and I am instructed to walk slowly past the length of the table. Some of the girls think the way this is done is "gross" and "chauvinistic." Others think it's fun, a chance to sashay and flirt. Sashaying and flirting don't come easy to me, and I'm nervous. At least every girl here isn't a "blue-eyed blonde." And several others, like me, are definitely over twenty-six. And none of us has a name; we have been reduced to a number.

* * *

Three days later we assemble again in the Help's Hall, this time in street clothes, to receive our shift assignments. I'm curious to see what I'll get. Whatever it is, I'm sure I'll make more money than I did at the Jungle Club, but I can't imagine how much more that might be.

By now I've heard about the "stars" of the Las Vegas cocktail waitress world: Nancy Lamb is the ex-wife of somebody in the prominent Lamb family—Ralph Lamb is the Clark County Sheriff and Floyd Lamb is the Nevada State Senator.

Blowsy blonde Stella Bramlet is the ex-wife of Al Bramlet, the powerful union organizer who's been secretary-treasurer of Culinary Workers Local 226 since 1954. Bramlet's a well-known, popular figure in town, a guy with a sense of humor who shmoozes well and is seen at all the charity events. The City of Hope, with a sponsoring committee made up of hotel executives, has just honored Bramlet at its annual banquet. In a juice town like Las Vegas, with Stella's union "connection," when the girls talk about her they assume she'll get the best shift—swing in the Dice Pit.

One by one our names are called. We are handed folded strips of paper. I open mine and read, "Keno Lounge. Day shift." This means I'll be giving away free drinks, rather than working in one of the cash bars where you have to keep track of the tabs for different tables, collect money and run credit card payments.

I'm pleased with this. It sounds easy. And I like the day shift, 1 a.m. to 7 p.m., because it means I'll have evenings free to be with Del.

Stella Bramlet, shoulders shrouded in a fat mink coat, unfolds and reads her piece of paper. Whatever she expected, it appears that she didn't get it. Her frown hardens her face. She tears the paper into tiny bits and flings them into the air with great drama. Her mouth tight, she sashays out of the room, mink coat swinging. We never see her again.

The porte-cochere of the MGM Grand Hotel

## CHAPTER 8 – A grand opening

When I tell Del my Keno Lounge shift assignment, he says, "I know you're disappointed not to get a pit shift."

In fact, I'm not disappointed. "I have no juice," I remind him. "I never expected to get a pit assignment. I'm happy to have a day shift, and a kind of normal working life. I don't know anything about the game of Keno, but so what? We're giving away free drinks. No bar checks, no money to change, no charges to get signed."

"Still, you'd make more money in the pit," he says.

What I'm hearing is that *he* is disappointed I didn't get a pit station.

Wednesday, December 5, 1973 is the big day, the culmination of nineteen months of race-speed construction. At 6 p.m. Klieg lights stab the desert sky, announcing the official opening, as if everyone in town didn't already know this was happening.

Fred MacMurray, Barbara Eden, and Jane Powell perform the ribbon-cutting ceremony that heralds the month-long opening celebration, which Del and I watch on television.

It would have been exciting to be there to see it all first hand, but Del informs me, "I'm not going down there and fight those crowds on the Strip just to see some new lights go on."

Since the hotel is opening in the evening, my first work shift will be the next day.

KORK radio's Red McIlvaine, through loudspeakers at the entrance, announces celebrities as they arrive in vintage cars: Cary Grant, June Haver, Hugh O'Brien, Vince Edwards, Britt Ekland, Howard Keel, Foster Brooks, Robert Conrad, Shirley MacLaine, Shecky Greene, George Raft, Herb Eden, Margaret O'Brien, Peter Lind Hayes, Mary Healy, Telly Savalas, Gordon MacRae, Phil Harris, Bobby Rydell, (Bernie) Allen and (Steve) Rossi, James Farentino, Sergio Franchi, Richard Roundtree, Dick Martin, June Allyson, Jackie Cooper, Peter Lawford, Connie Stevens, Jack Nicholson, Johnny Carson.

Las Vegans crowd the entry to get a glimpse of these people; they've never seen so many celebrities at one time. Neither have I, and I lived next door to Hollywood.

The Black Tie guests attend a dinner show in the 1200-seat Celebrity Showroom. They view a film clip from the MGM movie *Grand Hotel*. The Kessler Twins warm up the audience with a song and dance act and Cary Grant introduces the opening star, Dean Martin. Dean has his trademark drink in hand and make-believe stumble in his step.

He quips, "I love Las Vegas so much I'd work here without pay—and I'll give you odds that it turns out that way." Opening day glitches for any business become legendary; Dean jokes that he spent twenty minutes in the shower—and then the water came on. He announces that after opening night, Joan Rivers and Sergio Franchi will headline the Celebrity Showroom.

Meanwhile, in the main ballroom there's a VIP cocktail party with Nevada politicians, judges, businessmen, hotel execs and the media. They will see Dean Martin's second show. On every TV station, commentators throw around words like "glamour", "artistry", "excitement", "opulent", and "super-spectacular", which are repeated the following day in the newspapers.

There's no arguing this resort is big: a 5,000-seat grand ballroom with 300 miles of drapes, 2,100 rooms, 923 slot machines, thirteen crap tables, five entertainment lounges, five dining rooms, four roulette wheels, fifty Blackjack, seven Poker, five Pan, two Baccarat, a Keno lounge and two Big Six games. And forty-four marble columns. There is 145,000 square feet of convention space.

Did I mention the 300,000 plumbing fixtures?

Thousands of employees. I'm thinking there are probably hundreds of thousands of MGM lion logos, displayed everywhere, even in the carpeting design. Hardly seems enough. We're talking big numbers here. Eat your heart out, Caesars Palace.

Touted as a self-sufficient resort, The MGM Grand Hotel occupies 2.5 million square feet of space, including a twenty-six-story "T"-shaped tower with curtain walls of glass. The original construction budget is $75 million and overruns hover at $30 million. The *Las Vegas Review-Journal* reports that MGM plans to recover "$10 million a year in net profits after taxes from the hotel's gaming casino, largest in the world."

"That casino's bigger than a football field," Del says.

Below the casino, on the street level, are fancy shops that make up a 75,000 square-foot shopping arcade and in the first movie theatre ever built inside a hotel, 300 people can be seated in lounges and love-seats with cup-holders for drinks served by cocktail waitresses. The marketing plan is to run a series of MGM classics for the first two months: *An American in Paris, San Francisco, The Great Caruso, The Yearling, The Great Ziegfeld, Pat and Mike, National Velvet* and, of course, *Grand Hotel.*

At the east end of the shopping arcade is a Jai-alai fronton with pari-mutuel betting that seats 2,200 to watch the world's fastest game. I've never before heard of Jai-alai, and I can't wait to see it.

Scheduled to open later in December in the Ziegfeld Room, the 900-seat second main showroom, is a production show—every major hotel has one—called "Hallelujah Hollywood." In fact, the show is delayed and doesn't open until the following May, when it features Gary Marshall, Siegfried and Roy and Tanya the Elephant.

Del explains that casino execs call this all-encompassing plan of marketing, "the stick factor." He says, "The idea is that you give your customers everything they can possibly want on your property so they won't stray next door to your competition."

The MGM Grand Hotel has a $120 million-dollar advertising budget to assure that their customers know where they belong. And that is not kitty-corner at Caesars Palace.

* * *

At the end of my first day, Del waits outside the employee entrance in the yellow Mustang to drive me home.

"Enjoy that new casino smell," he says, "because cigarettes and spilled drinks'll soon make it smell just like all the rest of 'em."

I collapse into the passenger seat and burst forth the tears I've been holding back for the past hour.

"I can't do this," I wail. "My feet are killing me. This isn't like working 6 p.m. to 2 a.m. in L.A., where the last few hours you just serve a few drinks and get to sit down. These people *always* want drinks. The Keno lounge was full. We never stopped running back and forth to the bar—eight hours straight in these fucking heels."

Del's words of comfort and encouragement are, "Just one more day. Give it just one more day."

Four days in a row I cry and whimper and complain, and he repeats, "Try it just one more day." By the fifth day, the crowds either lessen or I'm getting used to it. I keep going back, but I'm really ready for my first two days off.

The black, three-inch, strappy, open-toed sandals that are required "dress issue" for the cocktail waitresses come from the shoe store downstairs in the shopping arcade. They seem cheap and not well made. They don't fit well and after eight hours my feet are numb. I'm not the only cocktail waitress who hates them.

On each side of the long counter where the Keno writers write the tickets are doors that lead into hallways behind the lounge. We cocktail waitresses who work the Keno Lounge are allowed to go back behind the closed doors and rest on stools for a few minutes. One day while I'm seated there I look up to read the bulletin board of hotel announcements. On a big, white piece of paper is typed,

"Employees are forbidden to wear to work tennis shoes, moccasins, and open-toed sandals."

So does this mean that these open-toed high heels that are killing my feet are "forbidden?"

Normally, my first impulse would be to march right down to the bar office, notice in hand, and make an indignant complaint. But this time I'm smart enough to keep my mouth shut. Maybe it's because I'm making such good money, and the thirty-day trial period isn't over yet.

We suffer these shoes for about a month before this requirement ends. I don't know why management changes their minds about these open-toed high heels, but it may have something to do with conflicting company policy. But maybe I'm giving management too much credit.

At the end of the third week the MGM is open I say to Del, "I never met so many stupid men in positions of authority."

\* \* \*

In the dressing room before the day shift, everyone buzzes over which girls have been the lucky five chosen to work the prestigious twenty-sixth floor penthouse Metro Room. This is an exclusive little casino established for high rollers—I've learned these big money gamblers are called "whales"—who want to gamble in private.

Evelyn tells us, "The hotel rents out suites on that floor for $1,000 a night."

The costumes for the cocktail girls in the Metro Room are much different from those for us casino girls. A twenty-sixth floor girl wears black stockings, black panties severely cut up the sides to the waist, and a black satin jeweled tux jacket that snaps only at the waist. No bra. And the requisite black high heels, of course.

In the Keno Lounge, there are four of us scheduled to work the day shift. One is scarlet-haired Dorothy. She has come to the MGM from working cocktails at the Aladdin. She seems confident and to know her way around the business.

"Call me Dor," she says. "Like the door to your dreams. Everyone does."

Dor looks at one of the girls being fitted by Evelyn for the Metro Room costume and whispers, "Can you imagine your tits in there? If you had to lean over, you'd have one hanging out."

For sure, it would be a challenge to move around in that costume, but the Metro Room assignment is purported to be *the* prestige job.

In spite of the short-waisted bustier, I like the red bellboy costumes we wear. I'm happy to be able to buy any kind of black stockings I want; the Bunny pantyhose we were required to buy from the Club were trash, running at the first brush of anything.

I'm pulling up my black stockings when one of the girls tells us that all the waitresses in Pit One—considered the casino "high roller" pit because of its highest minimum bet—campaigned heavily to be selected to work upstairs in the Metro Room. The whispered consensus is that the girls chosen to work the Metro Room are sleeping with bosses, and most likely will be sleeping as well with the whales.

Luckily, the five Metro girls have different shift hours from ours. The other four won't arrive till after we're dressed and on the floor, so they won't hear any of this catty gossip. The girl Evelyn's fitting either doesn't hear us whispering about her, or she doesn't care. Her posture is aloof, and she makes no eye contact with anyone.

In a newspaper interview, executive vice-president Bernie Rothkopf has stated that the twenty-sixth floor Metro Room is an "exclusive private membership club." The minimum bet at any table or game is $25.

Dor is skeptical. "Use your common sense," she says. "What would you do up there all day? How many high rollers can you have in one day? How many whales do you get with that kind of money that want to just gamble? Those girls are there for more than that."

With care she adjusts the red bellboy cap on her head at the exact correct angle. "I talked to one of them and they get paid an awful lot. I'm telling you, it's like the old days up there, when the bosses would tell you, go up to room so-and-so. Those girls were hired just for that."

This fancy, private twenty-sixth floor casino turns out to be short-lived.

Del informs me, "The Nevada Gaming Control Board made them close it because it's illegal in Nevada to have a private casino."

Now wouldn't you think the MGM bosses would know that up front, before they went to all the expense of outfitting the place?

I think it failed because there was no business. It just wasn't popular with the whales. From what I've seen so far in Vegas, big gamblers don't want to gamble in private. They like an audience— it makes them feel important, like they are appearing in the movie, *Ocean's Eleven.*

All but one of the girls who worked in the Metro Room just disappear; they never come back into the casino. Only one comes downstairs to take the most prestigious pit station, the Dice Pit, and she's not talking.

"That's because it wasn't a cocktail job to begin with," Dor declares. "Because why wouldn't those girls all take jobs downstairs afterwards?"

\* \* \*

December is the dead of winter in the high desert, and from one end to the other the cavernous casino is drafty and frigid.

The first week the MGM is open a few girls come up the escalator to the casino wearing coats over their costumes. Nobody has name tags and nobody knows who anybody else is, and there are a lot of cocktail waitresses.

These girls have signed in downstairs with the bar office, and now leave by the Flamingo entrance for the duration of their shift. Seven hours later they come back, go downstairs to the bar office, sign out and go home.

The pit floormen have no idea how many cocktail waitresses have been assigned to their individual pit. As long as they can get their coffee and drinks served to their players, they don't notice or care which "number" girl serves them.

I guess the girls figure they will wait till attrition thins the number of cocktail waitresses, and begin work when they have a better chance of making more tips.

* * *

I get my drinks for the Keno Lounge at the same bar that services four blackjack pits. Because it also services a little lounge with drinks and fresh seafood cocktails, it's called the Reef Bar.

In the service area of the Reef Bar some sort of leak floods the floor. Soon the soles of our high-heeled shoes—the ones we are now buying anywhere we like, in whatever style we like—are soaked. Now our feet are wet as well as cold. The service area smells like wet dog. When I peel off my pantyhose at the end of the shift, my feet are stained black.

My partners in the 320-seat Keno Lounge are red-haired Dor, Alice and Julie, a girl with a noticeable odor problem. We nickname her, "Stinky." Alice is a short brunette in her mid-thirties, square-faced with big breasts, so she looks cute in the costume. Julie, with a soft, wispy look, is quite pretty once you get past her smell.

Dor confides that she's confused about why she's been assigned the Keno Lounge when she should be in one of the 21 pits.

"I wasn't even going to apply for this job, but my friend told me he knows the bar manager, who owes him a favor, and he'd make sure I was hired with a good job. When I met Lenny everything was fine. He admitted he owes my friend and told me I'd have a pit job." Dor's friend is Jimmy Don, casino manager at the Aladdin.

"What do you think happened?" I ask.

In a cheery voice she says, "I can only guess it's because I didn't have the money. I didn't give anything. It was just a friend with a friend."

I don't know what she's talking about. "What money?"

"Some girls put in money to buy jobs here. Oh yes, and juice, and screw this one and that. That's how the jobs were obtained."

"I don't have juice," I say, "and I didn't pay, and I didn't screw anybody."

She gives me a knowing smile. "And look where you are."

* * *

As members of the bar part of the Food and Beverage Department we answer to Bar Manager Lenny Agnello; as workers in the Keno Lounge we answer to Tony DiIorio, the Keno Manager. Tony is none other than the short Italian with the fat sideburns who interviewed me at the Convention Center.

Tony remembers me and, because I'm much taller than he, jokes, "I'm going to get a ladder so I can go up on you." I like Tony because he's always in a good mood, so I'm not offended.

Neither Lenny nor Tony has given us any guidance as to how to work the three sections of the Keno lounge. We girls confer and divide the seats into four stations, which we agree to work in rotation.

Julie is easy to get along with, but it seems like she won't do anything about that heavy, intense smell, like a cross between rotten fish and dog shit.

"I don't think she ever washes," Alice says. "You can see she doesn't shave her armpits."

Dor says, "Evelyn is going to talk to her."

In retrospect, I wonder if Julie might have been one of those people who have a chemical imbalance in their body that results in a disagreeable odor. The condition, *trimethylaminuria*, is a rare genetic disorder where stomach bacteria don't metabolize the choline found in most foods. Sadly, there is no cure.

Two weeks later, when Julie gets fired Dor and Alice and I happily divvy up the lounge's three sections into three cocktail stations. With more seats each to service now, our daily tips will increase.

* * *

In slow-moving games like Baccarat, pretty girls in elegant dress are hired by hotels to work as shills. The shill working the day shift in the MGM's Baccarat pit looks like something out of a cheap men's magazine: spangled gown, mink stole, troweled make-up, and fat, bouffant curls that look suspiciously like a wig. Lara, the cocktail waitress in Baccarat, calls her, "Sophia Loren."

Days go by with no action in Baccarat, and I can understand how "Sophia Loren" could become crazed with boredom. At the end of each shift, she can hardly walk upright in her high heels. Whether she's doing drink or pills, or both, she's a mess.

One evening at the end of the day shift I'm behind her in the security time office as she clocks out. I follow her out the door. I watch her stagger across the pavement to where Del's waiting in the yellow Mustang, motor running. She opens the door, gets inside, and quickly gets out again, a dazed look on her face.

When I get into the car, my soldier-of-fortune looks like jalapeño jelly.

"What happened?" I ask.

He shakes his head. "I don't know, but she scared me to death."

The Lone Palm Trailer Park in the snow

Our trailer in the snow

## CHAPTER 9 – My Del, the spy

New Year's morning, 1974 I awaken, roll over and peek out the window. The world beyond is white and moving with fat, lazy snowflakes.

"Oh, my God, it's *snowing*!"

Del grumbles into his pillow. "Don't be silly. It never snows in Vegas."

The *Las Vegas Sun* reports a record-breaking eight inches, which takes three beautiful, clear, sunny days to melt.

Jack Binion leaves the Horseshoe to spend a month on his family's Montana ranch. As soon as he's gone, little brother Ted fires Del. In his chronic, drug-induced state of paranoia and aware of Del's government undercover drug-hunter background, Teddy Binion is certain Del has been placed by the feds at the Horseshoe intentionally to spy on and bust him.

Del is both pissed and amused. He has no respect for him, but Ted Binion's the man in charge while Jack is gone. There isn't anything Del can do about it until Jack returns from Montana.

* * *

We have bought a second car, a little red and white Ford. Del gets a call from a black baccarat cocktail waitress at the Tropicana. This is a girl Del knew years ago. A single mom, she wants to borrow money. He says she's also a hooker. Vegas is such a small town— officially 273,000—I'm not surprised he'd run into her again. She offers her two-year-old navy blue Cadillac as collateral. But she'll still need wheels to get to work, so Del gives her less money and the Ford to drive till she can pay him back.

Now he has no job, but he's driving a Cadillac.

Through Neil, Del has two new friends, Deputy District Attorney Jeff Silver, and District Court Judge in Department 10, Paul Goldman. All of them share the same wicked sense of humor. Like me, they love Del's stories of travel, undercover work, luck and adventure.

Jeff Silver, in his early thirties, is single and has shoulder-length dark hair, matching mustache, and an extensive collection of long-sleeved flowered shirts. When he discovers I'm an artist he tells me his living room is an art gallery, but not really.

"It's what I tell artists so they'll loan me their work to hang in the house," he says. This way, he can enjoy a rotating collection of original art. I think he's kidding, but I don't know him well enough to be sure.

Paul Goldman is older, Brooks-Brothers handsome despite a receding hairline. He wears large-lensed, wire rim glasses that enhance his intelligent look. Paul is married and has three young daughters.

When Paul complains about his bailiff, Neil tells Del and a plot is hatched.

"Paul's bailiff is stealing money from the purses of the secretaries in the courthouse," Neil explains. "He's using it to waltz a mistress. Paul knows it, but he can't catch him."

I wonder what sort of mistress would be impressed with purse change.

Del grins. "If I catch him, can I have his job?"

"Don't see why not. I'll check with Paul."

Paul and Jeff love the idea. In one of the secretary's purses Del, with Neil's help, plants money dusted with some stuff that collects fingerprints. The bailiff is caught, and Paul gives him the choice of resigning or being fired. The bailiff resigns, leaves town, and becomes the Chief of Police in Moab, Utah.

Del gets his job. Right away he tells Paul, "I'm gonna do whatever you tell me to do, boss. So be sure you're clear on what you want before you give me instructions. If you tell me to shoot a guy, I'm not gonna ask questions, I'm just gonna shoot him."

This kind of straight talk impresses Paul. I think he sees in Del the soldier-of-fortune he would like to be. Married, with kids, glasses, thin hair and a respectable job, there's no way Paul will ever lead the sort of life Del has had. Now, like Bill at the Lone Palm, he can do it vicariously.

Del in his bailiff's uniform, *sans* smile

One day Del comes home from work with an important announcement: "We've hired the first woman bailiff in the Clark County Courthouse."

When I meet the woman, Kathy Baldinado, I discover a stocky girl who wears her dark hair in an attractive page-boy style and looks pretty serious in her custom-tailored bailiff's uniform. The judges, Del, and the other bailiffs refer to Kathy Baldinado as "no balls 'dinado." Not always behind her back.

Women haven't really "come a long way, baby", and I think she knows she has no choice but to treat it as the kind of hearty joke that comes with being the courthouse's first female bailiff.

* * *

Several months later Del's friend, the Tropicana Baccarat waitress/hooker, calls to ask if she can have her '70 Caddy back.

By now, I'm driving the Caddy every day to work at the MGM, and I like it. It's true what they say about that Cadillac feel. She doesn't have the money to repay Del, and her kids have trashed the interior of the Ford. Del says, no, and it's the last we see of her and of the Ford.

Then one day Del tells me, "I got a chance to buy a red Mercedes convertible from a guy who's behind in his car payments."

Wheeling and dealing appeals to Del, who has mastered the art. He likes to help people out and get a deal in the bargain.

I've never driven a Mercedes before, and no matter how little he paid for it, I can't get past the idea that this is an expensive car. What if I wreck it? What if in the Mayfair supermarket parking lot I get a ding on the door? I'm too nervous in that car to be a good driver. I'm perfectly happy to let him drive the Mercedes to and from work. I'll stick with my big Caddy.

Neil and Jeff and Paul tease Del about driving such a high profile car on a District Court bailiff's salary. Del finally sells it— at a profit—because it's "too conspicuous for a bailiff to drive."

* * *

Once a year the legal secretaries put on a fund-raising roast of all the judges in town. It's a big social event and Del and I are invited.

For me, the highlight of the evening is when attorneys Tom Severns and Ted Embry sing a satirical song they have written for Nevada's Lieutenant Governor Harry Reid. I will never forget these words from the chorus, *"Harry Reid—nothing tickles like a hairy reed..."*

## CHAPTER 10 – Day shift, play shift

Below the MGM Grand casino and behind the Shopping Arcade is a maze of service hallways, dressing rooms, offices, break rooms, storage, maintenance areas, kitchens, and the Help's Hall. Because there is a pervasive stale smell and no windows, the employees now call this entire network "mole city."

From the Lone Palm Motel and Trailer Park, an eight-minute drive down the Strip gets me to the MGM employee parking lot at 10:30 a.m. I allow myself two minutes to park the Caddy and walk to the employee's entrance, two minutes to clock in at the Security Window, three minutes to sign in at the bar manager's office, and fifteen minutes in the dressing room.

That's just enough time to gossip, change into my black stockings, red panties, bustier dress, collar and cuffs and adjust my pillbox hat. The forehead dip in the edge of the hat is required to be exactly one inch above my left eyebrow.

At eight minutes to eleven, Dor blows in. "Running late," she mutters. "Heavy drama at home."

"What happened?" I ask.

"Oh, my kid's hysterical." Dor is a single mom with a seven-year-old daughter. "In the middle of the night the cat ate the gerbil—guts and blood all over the place."

She's breathing hard as she hurries into her costume, and we leave the dressing room at the same time. Going up the escalator to the casino, an elderly lady behind her says, "Miss, miss, do you know you don't have any underwear on?"

In her haste Dor has pulled on her black stockings and forgotten the red panties. At the top of the escalator she makes a u-turn and takes the down escalator back to the dressing room. This makes her late on the floor.

The bar department—Lenny Agnello's domain—has a system of pink warning slips to issue when a cocktail waitress breaks rules. After the first thirty days the MGM is open, the ruling system will be two warning slips for the same infraction and they can fire you. This has been worked out to document your misbehaviors so that when you're fired, the hotel doesn't get in trouble with the culinary union.

"Be happy you have a union behind you to guarantee your job," Del says. "Those floormen and casino bosses can be fired at the drop of the hat, and they know it. It's what makes them cranky."

In Seattle, my father was a laundry truck driver and member of the Teamsters' Union. One of his best customers was Dave Beck, a former laundry truck driver himself, who served as president of the International Brotherhood of Teamsters from 1952 until 1957 when he was succeeded by Jimmy Hoffa. In 1959 Beck was prosecuted for embezzlement and labor racketeering, convicted on federal charges of income-tax evasion, served thirty months at McNeil Island Penitentiary, and later was pardoned by Washington State Governor Albert Rosellini.

I grew up in the shadow of the Teamsters' Union and their wonderful benefits that paid for my mother's chronic illnesses and surgeries. So I already harbor a favorable feeling for the Las Vegas Culinary Union.

Alice and I are amazed that Dor doesn't get a warning slip for being late. Instead she gets called into the Bar Manager's office for something that sends her back to the floor pissed off.

Lately, with some regularity she's been called out of the Keno Lounge to fill in when the pit is short a waitress. Her juice, Jimmy Don, has told her, "Lenny'll put you there when he can, because he owes me a big favor. Just let me know how everything's going."

Dor tells us about this visit to Lenny's office, where the air is heavy with smoke from the cigars he favors. Behind closed doors he said, "After you get off work, maybe we could have some drinks or something."

Dor thought he was just being friendly, and then she realized that he meant if she continues to work in the pit she'll "owe him."

"I have a boyfriend," she told him.

Through cigar-clenching teeth, he said, "This has nothing to do with your boyfriend."

She thought it best to be straight with him. "Lenny, I'm not going to sleep with anybody for a pit job. It isn't worth it."

"It isn't?" He blew a big puff of smoke.

"No."

"Well, it will be."

*Agnello* is the Italian word for lamb, but this *agnello* is turning out to be the wolf.

After relating this event in Lenny's office, Dor tells Alice and me that she's resigned to the fact that she probably won't be working any longer in the pit. She plans to stay, as much as she can, out of the bar manager's way.

"Do you believe him? Wanting me to do something like that?" Dor laughs as she garnishes an old-fashioned, twisting the sliced orange just so. "He as much as told me that if I sleep with him I can be in the pit all the time and have a good job."

Alice, who's shorter than Dor and actually about Lenny's height, says, "Well, what's wrong with that?"

* * *

At the service bar in the Reef Lounge the water leak has been fixed, but Ronni discovers a hole in the floor the size of a cocktail olive. You can look right down through it and see the parking garage below.

Ronni is the pretty blond waitress whose station is the Oyster Bar section of the Reef Lounge. She serves drinks and jumbo-sized shrimp and crab cocktails and plates of fresh-shucked oysters. Because this is a cash area, she has to bring a couple of hundred dollars to work every day to use as a bank; she has to pay for the drinks and seafood, then serve and collect from the customers.

Lily and Arline, the two girls who service the closest 21 pit—Pit Two—also get their drinks from the Reef service bar. Lily, just turned twenty-one, wears rose-colored, heart-shaped glasses and has a nonsensical sense of humor. Her father is a prominent Las Vegas chiropractor. Arline is older, in her late thirties, a single mom with two children who reads the *Wall Street Journal* and the humor of James Thurber and S.J. Perelman, who she informs us "wrote a lot of the Marx Brothers movies."

Lily and Arline and I peer down the hole Ronni shows us. You can actually see guys moving around in the parking garage. Next day Lily brings in fishing line and paper. On the little pieces of paper the girls write naughty messages like "I need a good tongue-licking" and "I want to suck your cock." They attach a note to the fishing line and stuff note and line through the hole to dangle into the garage.

They wait. If someone doesn't come along right away and see the note, they jiggle the line. It catches the attention of one of the parking lot attendants. He snatches the note and looks up at the garage ceiling to see where the fishing line is coming from. His expression says the floor is thick enough that he can't hear the laughing and giggling above him. He walks away, taking the note with him.

Into the hole the girls lower a line with a new note. Another attendant discovers it, looks up, frowns, and jams it into his shirt pocket.

A half hour later, three uniformed parking lot attendants appear at the casino's Flamingo entrance.

"Whoa," Arline says with a snicker. "Here they come."

At the head of the stairs leading down to the Cub bar, slot machines and gaming tables, the three guys scan the casino.

Lily laughs, adjusts her heart-shaped glasses, and says, "They're trying to match the floor plan here with the parking garage. They're trying to figure out where the hole is in the floor to see where the notes are coming from."

This sexual silliness goes on for a week, driving the parking attendants crazy. Then the maintenance men come, fill in the hole in the Reef Bar service area, and lay a new rubber mat.

* * *

In our trailer over coffee one morning, Del tells me a casino joke: "*Cocktail waitress* is Greek for *alcoholic*."

The cocktail waitresses who work days at the MGM not only consider themselves privileged, but also "normal." Most of the girls have young children in school, and for that reason requested to be assigned the day shift. The consensus is that those girls who work the swing shift are "the worst"; rumors abound about how they stagger out of the hotel at 4 a.m.—the end of their shift—in a drunken stupor.

As I get to know Ronni I learn she graduated from Valley High School, is married with three children, and her husband works as a Maitre d' in the Stardust showroom. Ronni and I discover that we both like arts and crafts, and a new bond of friendship begins. I'm attracted by her positive personality and sense of wit and humor.

It's a quiet afternoon in the casino. Ronni and Dor and I spend a lot of time in the Reef Bar service area. There is what in the cocktail trade is called "side work" that always needs to be done. While the bartender prepares and pours alcoholic and soft drinks, we are responsible for preparing coffee and keeping hot water for tea at the boil.

We garnish the drinks, and must let the bar boy know if we are short on napkins, rubber bands, ash trays or highball glasses. Dor has taught Ronni and me how to "diaper" the highball glasses in which we serve hot coffee or tea: you wrap a cocktail napkin around the glass and secure it with a rubber band. When it's busy, it's much easier to set up a coffee drink if there is already a row of diapered glasses ready.

She has also shown us how to properly clean an empty coffee carafe—you rub the inside with a lime wedge that's been dipped in salt. Ashtrays are emptied and wiped clean with a wet cocktail napkin.

On this slow afternoon, we exchange stories as we try to look busy.

"When I was sixteen," Ronni says. "Wayne Newton lived in my neighborhood. He was appearing with his brother at the Fremont. They were 'The Newton Brothers.'"

"Really?" I ask. "Wayne Newton? What was he like?"

"Kind of dorky. He was eighteen and dating my friend, Donna Giuffre."

Dor explains to me, "Donna's the daughter of Gus Giuffre, the guy on TV."

Ronni continues: "But Donna was in love with Wayne's brother, Jerry. We were all in love with Jerry. We were at their house a lot. But then Wayne got his hit with 'Danke Schoen', dumped Jerry and moved out of the neighborhood."

Another girl who went to Las Vegas High with Ronni is Arline younger sister, blond Angie, who works in Pit One, the high-roller blackjack pit where the minimum bet is $25.

"Angie talked me into applying," Ronni tells me. "She coached me on everything from how to flirt to how to put on make-up and how to walk sexy. She loaned me a low-cut black dress slit all the way up to here." She gestures at her thigh.

While we stand in the service area and talk, we keep an eye out for Milton, Lenny's assistant. He gets grouchy if he thinks we're goofing around.

Ronni adds, "Angie took me to the Boulevard Mall to shop for a bra that made me look like I have tits, and it cost an atrocious price."

She tells us how Angie piled her long blond hair on top of her head.

"I didn't even look like me," Ronni says, "When I looked in the mirror I didn't see me."

Though Ronni had never worked cocktails before, the only hang-up Angie saw to Ronni being hired at the MGM was that Ronni walked like a duck, her feet pointed out.

"She put me in high black heels and schooled me for a whole day on how to walk in those things. Then at the interview I was concentrating on how Angie told me to put one foot in front of the other, and I stepped on my own foot and fell flat on my face. Honestly!"

This image sends us into a lengthy laugh.

"I heard Angie in the hallway scream '*shit!*', and I just got up and said, 'Well, somebody told me if you wanted a job here you had to make a noble entrance, and here I am.'"

"Did they know you didn't have any experience?" I ask.

"Nah, when they asked me about my experience I lied through my teeth with a smile on my face. I told them I had all kinds of cocktail experience, that my uncle owned a bar in Chicago. I whipped a name right off the top of my head. I told 'em I'd worked back there for him during the summer, and once you hustle cocktails in a bar you can hustle cocktails anywhere. I guess they bought it because they hired me."

"It's not like they give you a test to see if you know drinks," Dor says. "They only care that you're pretty."

Now Ronni has thirty days to prove herself. I admire her moxy.

She continues: "I had to have Angie go with me to get my tray, because I didn't know what to buy." Unlike the Playboy club, the MGM does not provide us with cocktail trays.

Ronni has juice she hasn't used. She worked the front desk at Circus Circus, where MGM Food and Beverage Manager Danny Litwack worked.

"I didn't tell Danny I was coming over to the MGM as a cocktail waitress 'cause, until the actual day I went to work, I didn't believe I was really going to do it."

Vegas being a small town, Ronni's also acquainted with Stella Bramlet. "She's not very well-liked," she confides. "People talked about her, how she was juiced in and wouldn't last, which she didn't. Remember how she threw away her station assignment before we even opened? Anyway, she looked old to me, with that reddish brown hair all ratted out."

Ronni finds the bar manager, Lenny Agnello, disgusting. "From the very first time I saw him—he came walking up, puffing his cigar—I didn't like him."

She's not surprised to hear that Lenny propositioned Dor and respects Dor for saying, no.

"He's so full of shit, you could give him an enema and bury him in a shoebox," Ronni says.

"Amen," Dor says as she leaves the service station to make a round through the Keno Lounge to see if anybody wants a drink.

Ronni confides to me that Angie is having simultaneous affairs with a Vegas advertising agency owner and Tropicana Hotel owner Deil Gustafson, and is also sleeping with Danny Litwack. "That's why Angie got Pit One," she says.

Our new friendship strengthens when Ronni confesses that she too cried on the first few days at the end of her shift because her feet hurt.

\* \* \*

The bartender at the Casino Bar, where the Pit One girls have their service bar, is chisel-faced, happy-go-lucky Kevin.

"I dated him in high school," Ronni says.

Kevin swears he doesn't remember any "dates," per se. But he remembers Ronni from Vegas High, and the two of them joke around a lot.

One day Kevin sees an opportunity for guy fun when he realizes Betty, the cash waitress in the Casino Bar Lounge, is a nice Mormon girl from Parawan, Utah.

Now, life in Las Vegas is heavily influenced by two factions: the mob and the Mormons.

Arline, who reads a lot and likes to quote statistics, says, "There are more churches here per capita than anywhere else in the country, and most of them are either Catholic or Latter Day Saints. Plus Las Vegas has the highest percentage of eye ulcers per capita in the nation."

"What do eye ulcers have to do with anything?" Ronni asks.

"Nothing. I just think it's interesting." Arline is a fountain of trivia. She goes on to explain that Mormon girls are famously reputed to be sheltered, gullible, and naïve to, "shall we say, the ways of the world."

Betty, recently married to a guy who works upstairs in the accounting department, proves to be no exception. She has just attended her first luau, and tells us, "Everybody dressed up in Hawaiian costumes, and they had this huge pit, and they had this whole pig in there, and they had him all spread out on this rack, and they buried it, and they cooked it for two days, and it was soooo good. It tasted like pork."

Today Betty and Ronni have been pulled out of their regular stations to relieve the pit girls when they take their union-contract-designated breaks. Kevin's on his third scotch since 11 a.m. and fascinated with Betty's naiveté.

Now, during our lunch break in the Help's Hall, Betty won't look at Ronni. Betty has tears in her eyes. Ronni puts her hand on Betty's arm. "Are you okay?"

Betty starts to cry, endangering her carefully-drawn eyeliner. "I feel so bad. Kevin told me what happened to you in high school. I think it's just terrible, and I just want you to know I'm so sorry."

After lunch, Ronni marches up to Kevin at the Casino Bar and demands, "What did you tell that little girl? She can't stop crying, for God's sake."

Kevin glances around to be sure no one of concern is watching, takes a drink, and laughs like hell. "You're kiddin'. She's really cryin'? I just wanted to get her going, maybe get her a little excited, you know? I didn't know it was going to upset her."

"What'd you tell her?"

"Oh, I just made up a story. I told her when you were in high school—remember how you loved football and basketball?—I told her that after football practice we picked you up and took you into the locker room and strapped you down to the table, and we all had our way with you." He chuckles and pours himself another scotch.

"She believes you, Kev."

"Nah, she doesn't."

"Yes, she does. You're trying to get her horny, and now she's upset and crying." Ronni is livid. "When she comes back out here, you tell her that story is not true, because she's going to be upset all day, and I have to work with her."

Betty approaches the bar, and Ronni doesn't wait for Kevin to speak. She tells Betty, "Kevin lied to you. That story about me in high school is not true. He just made it up."

A floorman calls Ronni into the pit to take a drink order. Kevin takes this chance to say to Betty, "Ronni is real upset that I told you. We'll just have to pretend that I didn't say anything."

Ronni returns to the bar with her drink order and Betty goes to stand by the entrance to the pit. Kevin winks at Ronni and whispers, "I told her that *you* wanted me to say it was a lie."

Betty never gets over her belief that twenty football players raped Ronni in the Valley High School locker room.

Despite Kevin's drinking problem, he's a terrific bartender. No matter how soused he is, he can pour faster than anybody. He never misses a drink, never spills a drop, never has to ask you to repeat any part of your order.

But one day at the Casino Bar Kevin is so drunk he collapses. Security guards come and call for paramedics. While we watch, they carry Kevin out of the casino on a stretcher.

I ask Angie what happened.

"Oh, it's terrible! He's having a malaria attack," she says. Two other girls nod.

When Del was a bush pilot in Brazil he had malaria and he has described to me the treatment, and the symptoms. Kevin hasn't exhibited any of the flu-like symptoms, such as fatigue, fever, muscle aches, chills, sweats, vomiting or, to my knowledge, diarrhea. Plus our desert environment is not known for mosquitos. Angie says, "He was pouring drinks fine one minute, and then he just fell over."

The following two days are Kevin's days off, and then he's right back at work as usual. Del scoffs at this malaria story. "Recovering from a malaria attack would take at least a couple of weeks to a month. The man simply got drunk and passed out."

I don't know if these casino people just don't know anything about malaria, or if they're covering for Kevin because they all like him. Either way, it's okay by me. Not my business to educate.

* * *

On the two days when Arline is off, Lily works with Rhonda. Rhonda is a statuesque blonde—my height—but with bad posture. She is terribly round-shouldered. I figure she either grew up uncomfortable with her height, or she is uncomfortable sticking out her chest. Either way, I think it's sad because she is such a beautiful girl.

When the twenty-sixth floor Metro Room was still open, we had some hot bathroom break gossip: two of the waitresses, one of them a former Miss Nevada, got into a fist fight over a tip. The former Miss N was fired and the other waitress, with strong juice, came downstairs to work in the Dice Pit. No one on day shift bid for either of these two Metro Room openings.

This could be because of the story Lara tells us about Kim, Rhonda and Lily and the Metro Room party:

Kim approaches Lara one day in the Baccarat pit, asks her what she's doing this evening, and extends an invitation: "Why don't you join me and my friends tonight? They have the whole twenty-sixth floor and the hotel's fixing a special gourmet buffet for them. We all went to school together, so it'll be a nice get-together—no hanky-panky, just come and have a nice dinner." She tells Lara that Lily and Rhonda will be there, too.

So will the six big Italian Baccarat players in flowered shirts and gold jewelry who have been tipping Lara all day.

That evening Lara arrives at the same time as Lily and Rhonda. Besides the chance for the free dinner—a girl's gotta eat, after all—they are curious about the twenty-sixth floor.

"Elegant, with a lot of white-and-gold leafing type stuff," Lara says. A Baccarat dealer she knows guides them to a long table, where every other seat is open. Among some of the other women, Lara recognizes a wild, crazy-mouthed hooker who frequents the beauty shop she uses.

Already uncomfortable, the girls take open seats. Lara notices all the women are blondes and all the men dark and "mafioso-looking." No sign of brunette Kim.

When Lily asks, one of the men says, "She might be a little late."

Lara speaks to the man on her right, who has put his arm around the back of her chair. "So you went to school with Kim?"

The Italian says, "What?"

"Kim told us you guys went to school together."

He says, "What, are you crazy?" He removes his arm.

Lara hears Rhonda say to the man next to her, "Well, I don't know, what do you want me to do, kiss your ring?"

The buffet is opened and the girls get up from the table to serve themselves. They notice the coffee tables around the room are scattered with bowls containing rocks of cocaine.

Lily excuses herself to go to the restroom. Rhonda and Lara follow.

Inside, Rhonda whispers, "Oh my God, what have we gotten ourselves into?"

"Remember," Lily says, "Kim said we're not obligated to do anything."

"Where the hell *is* Kim?" Rhonda wants to know.

Lara says, "Bleaching her hair?"

Rhonda says, "Let's get out of here."

They come out of the restroom just as a three-piece band is setting up. Lily recognizes a friend of her family's, orchestra leader

Henry Rose. He takes her aside and says, "This is not a nice place to be. If you don't leave, I'm going to tell your father."

"No, no, we're leaving," she whispers.

After the girls leave, the men watch the Superbowl, get mad at the television and throw it out of a window.

That night none of the girls ever see Kim.

* * *

The new girl in the Dice Pit doesn't talk about the 26th floor. Rumor has it that she "swings" with another girl and her husband. She does share with us a story about a player she went out with who gave her head while she was on her period. Now when this player shows up to play craps, behind his back the waitresses refer to him as, "Tomato Face."

One day, she tells him, "I can't fuck you. I just spent three days in bed with two guys and I'm sore on both ends."

She insists it's a joke. "Listen," she says, "the truth is, if I got as much action as everybody thinks I get, I wouldn't be able to drag myself out of the house and come to work."

## CHAPTER 11 – My Del, the bigamist

It looks like now Del and I will stay in Vegas indefinitely. We both have good jobs. Onto the front of the Wilderness he builds a sky-lighted living room, we buy a couch and build book shelves from wooden boards and cement blocks.

We are beginning to feel like part of the community.

\* \* \*

Del doesn't ask me formally to marry him. We have testing conversations in which we discuss how getting married would affect our lives.

"Would we stay in Las Vegas?"

"Would we buy a house?"

"Should we get married in a wedding chapel?" There are so many in Las Vegas from which to choose. "Which one?"

"Will we agree to sleep only with each other, or are certain 'friends' permitted?"

It's the 70s, after all, and these are important questions. "Open marriage" is all the rage among my generation. In later decades, this kind of thing would come to be called "polyamorous relationships."

These marriage discussions feel to me more business-like than romantic. But they appeal to my old German Lutheran upbringing about what's right—if you're going to live together, you really should be married. I suspect this appeals to Del's Catholic background, as well. Even though he has been married and divorced twice before, that doesn't concern me.

We're way too old to be concerned about religious differences. Del is not a practicing Catholic, nor am I a practicing Lutheran, other than my devotion to a mean casserole. Del has never had children and at forty-six, he declares, "No kids, okay?" I'm not one of those women who has dreamed about having children from the time they're little girls. I have always assumed it's just something you eventually do if you are a woman, like buying a bra. If Del doesn't want to have children, it's okay by me.

Even though I've always said, "Great adventures do not happen to married ladies," with Del I envision an exciting, adventure-filled married life. I figure this Vegas thing really is only temporary, and sharing my life with a man with his experience could lead to all kinds of creative and entrepreneurial activities.

So while he hasn't asked outright—and I haven't said yes outright—we set the date.

Del favors western attire: jeans, cowboy boots, cowboy hat, western shirts with pearl buttons. "I am not marrying a cowboy," I state.

So he lets me drag him down to Mr. B's Clothes For Men on Fremont Street to buy for the wedding a modern seventies suit, with light-colored stripes and wide lapels. He's skeptical and grumbles about how he looks in it. "Looks like a 'today' version of a Zoot suit."

We agree: no silly wedding chapel for us. Valentine's Day, February 14, 1974, we get married at the Clark County Courthouse. After the ceremony, we go with our two witnesses, Neil and Ronni, to Bob Taylor's Original Ranch House for a wedding dinner.

Bob Taylor's is a classic—since 1955—old Las Vegas steak house, advertised as, "A Supper Club." We drive forty-five minutes out two-lane Rancho Drive, which then becomes the Tonopah Highway. The restaurant sits back from the highway on Rio Vista Street, a dirt road. You can't miss it—in the middle of flat, boring desert the building is shaded in a grove of Chinese elms. In the distance, the ridges of the Sheep Mountain Range edge the horizon.

You can see that Bob Taylor's was originally a working ranch. Corrals surround the slumpstone ranch house. A fence made of logs and wagon wheels leads from the gravel parking area to the front door. Inside, the walls around the massive living room fireplace are decorated with colorful broadsides and black and white eight-by-ten movie stills from old westerns featuring Dale Robertson, Joel McCrea, Roy Rogers, Robert Dixson, Tom Mix and John Wayne. Western movie star and former Lieutenant

Governor Rex Bell dined here often with his silent-screen-star wife, Clara Bow.

My stomach growls at the smell of roasting steaks that wafts from the open grill. This getting-married business has made me ravenous.

Dining at Bob Taylor's Ranch House on my wedding day makes me feel like now I'm part of the history of Las Vegas.

* * *

Downtown near the courthouse Del and his friends Neil, Jeff and Paul lunch frequently at Max's Corned Beef Junction Deli Sandwich Shop.

Special combination and double-deck sandwiches are named after local policemen, lawyers and judges. Former Philadelphian and owner "Big Max" Corsun knows everybody. Reporters from the *Las Vegas Sun, Las Vegas Review-Journal*, and Bob Brown's *Valley Times* hang out here. Gossip and rumor circulates at Max C's to rival that in the MGM Grand casino.

Today the roving reporter for the *Las Vegas Sun* is lunching at Max C's. This reporter writes a column called, "*Man on the Street.*" He asks a question of the day and stops people in the street for answers. Their answers and pictures appear in the column.

Everyone is talking about how gas prices have risen dramatically. President Nixon has announced a "fuel crisis", and the nation's economy is reported to be going down the proverbial toilet. Every night for two months, in a show of saving energy, all the famous Las Vegas Strip hotels have doused their spectacular marquee lights.

The roving reporter targets Del in his bailiff's uniform for today's question, "What do you think the future holds for Las Vegas?"

Del laughs and says, "I hope it gets worse, so people who've saved their money can buy things cheap."

Click. Click. Photo and quote appear the next day in the morning *Sun*.

In the afternoon Del has just returned to the courthouse from lunch when he gets a phone call. A woman's voice he doesn't immediately recognize says, "Hi, this is Kay."

"Kay who?" he says.

"Your—wife—Kay."

"Oh, hi," he says. "Been a long time. Don't you mean *ex-wife*?"

"That's something we need to get straightened out," she says.

"What?"

Kay announces, "We need to get divorced."

Del tells me later that he really did think she was kidding. He says to her, "I thought we already *were* divorced. I was served."

She says, "I never went through with it." Read: *I never paid the lawyer.* "You went to South America, and I couldn't find you. I've been wondering how to get ahold of you. I didn't even know you were back in town. Then I saw your picture in the paper this morning."

Del is dumbstruck. He has illegally taken another wife.

I am married to a *bigamist*. In all my adventurous fantasies, I never imagined myself in this kind of situation. I never imagined myself married to a bigamist.

With no clue as to how to get out of this legal predicament, Del confides in Paul and asks his advice.

"Ha ha," says Paul. "Old enough to know better, young enough to do it again."

"This is *serious*," Del protests. "How do I fix this?"

Paul doesn't give an immediate answer. He sees a lot of humor in being "the only judge in the courthouse who has a bailiff with two wives."

Del has a fiercely serious side when it comes to law enforcement. He does not think this is the least bit funny.

Paul can't wait to call Jeff in the DA's office and Jeff can't wait to call Neil. Del's friends are delighted to have something this juicy to rag him with.

Finally Paul says the first thing that needs to be done is to annul Del's marriage to me. Then he will finalize the divorce with Kay. After that he will remarry us in a private ceremony in his chambers. Paul will see that all the papers are sealed by the court, never to become public.

Del appreciates that Paul has the answer to his problem, but when it comes to the execution, he gets a big surprise.

"We'll do the ceremony during the lunch hour," Paul says. "Jeff will come over and play the wedding march on his harmonica."

Del doesn't want what he perceives to be silly fanfare. "Can't we just do the paperwork and call it even?"

Paul smiles. "Oh no, we have to have a real wedding ceremony."

On the appointed day, I arrive at the courthouse in a not-too-sexy dress and present myself in Paul's chambers. Del, of course, is wearing his bailiff's uniform. Paul sports his black judicial robes. Jeff is ready with his harmonica.

"Smile, Del," Paul says. "You're getting married."

Del grumbles something about how it's not protocol to smile when you're wearing a military uniform. He tries to be serious, but Paul and Jeff are having way too much fun.

To begin the official wedding ceremony, Paul opens Kahlil Gibran's book *The Prophet* and reads the chapter on *Crime and Punishment*.

To the tune of the wedding march on the harmonica Del and I are—for the second time—pronounced man and wife.

## CHAPTER 12 – Tricks & tips

Since I have nothing to hide and I think the whole experience was funny and bizarre, I carry this story to work the next day to share with the girls. Arline is delighted to learn that my husband works for Paul Goldman. She wants me to introduce her.

"I follow him in the newspapers," she explains. "I've had a crush on him for years. You have to introduce me."

I am not going near this. "Arline, he's married."

She waves a dismissive hand. "Oh, I know that, but I could make him really happy." Her grin tells me she is thrilled at the idea.

"I am not introducing you. He doesn't need a sexy blonde who *reads* to complicate his life."

She gives me a playful jab in the arm. "Huh. Some friend you are."

"Just keep reading the newspaper."

\* \* \*

The amplified feminine voice echoes through the casino: "Paging Mr. Mehoff, Mr. Jack Mehoff."

The first time I hear this I am on my way to lunch. I look at the bank of house phones against the wall between the Reef Bar and the escalator, sure that one of my contemporaries is behind the joke. I know entertainers often have themselves paged, especially if they are appearing in the hotel, because the "name announcement" acts as free publicity.

But I am amazed that the switchboard girls are not hip to the "jack-me-off" joke.

The Culinary union contract says all cocktail waitresses get two ten-minute breaks and one forty-minute lunch break. Breaks are not always at the same time every day. If bar manager Lenny Agnello is mad at you, he tells the break girls to go to your station at a particular time, so that you arrive in the Help's Hall for lunch at the same time as the hotel maids. This guarantees you will spend more time waiting in the cafeteria line than eating. And after all, we are *MGM* cocktail waitresses—it is considered socially beneath our station in life to even speak to maids and porters. To have to stand in line with them for any length of time, in front of all the dealers and other employees in the Help's Hall, is humiliating.

We are allowed to carry onto the floor only a small bag with "essentials" like lipstick and pens, which we stash on a shelf under the bar while we work.

I also carry toothpaste and a toothbrush. I plan the actual eating of my lunch so that I come back up the escalator to the casino seven minutes before I have to sign back in. This gives me time to stop in the ladies room, pee, and brush my teeth. Unlike the dealers, cocktail waitresses do not have an official Break Room. So we have to share the ladies' restrooms with the tourists.

Today I am returning to the casino floor from lunch with Lily and Betty. We make our usual last-minute stop in the restroom near the Reef Bar.

I am brushing my teeth when I hear a woman's voice behind me speaking to another woman. "Oh, look, she brushes her teeth."

I raise my head from the sink, foam-mouthed, and stare at them. Do they really think that just because we are cocktail waitresses we do not brush our teeth like other people?

She raises her camera and snaps my picture.

I wave my toothbrush. "Hey, you can't take pictures."

She smiles. "I know you can't take pictures in the *casino*," she says, "but I thought it'd be okay in the bathroom."

I am stunned by this comment. What are these women thinking?

As we leave the bathroom to walk to the Reef Bar service station to check back in, Lily mutters, "Stupid tourists."

* * *

The working cocktail world of a Las Vegas casino is quite different from the working cocktail world of a Playboy Club.

Playboy advertises for girls with no waitressing experience. They want to train the Bunnies their way, and at the same time assure that girls don't come to the club with bad habits, like padding checks or not ringing up drinks and pocketing the money. In a Playboy Club, the Room Director handles the customer's final check; there is no opportunity to be tempted to steal.

In a hotel casino, where I now find myself, it looks like anything goes.

It is no secret that some of the girls who work the Parisian and Cub bars are stealing. For instance, if a player is on a comp—where the hotel picks up his room, food and beverages—and he is drinking heavily and running a tab, the waitress can add another party's drinks to his check. She collects from the other party and pockets the money.

Arline explains, "Comped players just sign. They almost never look at the check. What does he care how much it says? He's not paying."

She says sometimes a waitress with creative handwriting abilities will just sign the player's name to someone else's check. "Players move around. How does the hotel know where and how much he drank?"

In the service area, Arline shows Ronni and me how to sample a new drink you have never tasted. While you are still at the bar, "before you serve the drink to the customer, you insert a cocktail straw in it, plug one end with your finger, and extract the sample. You put the straw in your mouth, release your finger, and *voila!* a taste."

From Arline and Dor we learn there are ways to get revenge on a customer who is mean or giving you a hard time and not tipping. The most common is to squirt into the customer's drink a few drops of an odorless, tasteless eye-drop liquid, Visine. "This will give him the *real* squirts," Dor says. "Soon he'll be running with diarrhea for the bathroom, hopefully never to return."

Arline whispers, "It's illegal, but it's done all the time."

A "special" is when you add a shot of vodka to a player's beer. "He'll never taste it," Dor says, "and he'll get drunk so fast he'll either loosen up his pocket or he'll leave, making space for someone else who might be more generous."

Arline and Dor have worked cocktails for years, and they seem to know all the tricks.

"If a guy's drinking Bloody Marys, with your finger you rim the edge of the glass with Tabasco sauce. He won't taste it right away, but then his lips will start to burn and the more he licks them, the more they'll burn."

All these bad behaviors—just because somebody doesn't give you a tip. I can see how easy it would be, before long, to sell out your values for a dollar.

Arline entertains us with a story about when she worked the Baccarat pit at the Stardust. The player's bored girlfriend, seated behind him while he bet, kept demanding—never asking nicely—for Arline to bring her another Brandy Alexander.

"She's snotty and looks at me like I'm dirt," Arline says. "I take it for awhile, but then enough is enough, and she's getting worse as she gets drunk. It's time for her to go." Arline heavily laced the girlfriend's next Brandy Alexander with Pepto Bismol.

Girlfriend noticed the strange taste, got angry, called over the Baccarat floorman. "This waitress is trying to poison me!" she shouted. "Taste this! See for yourself!" She held out the drink, daring the floorman to respond.

The floorman accepted the drink, raised it to his lips, took a sip.

Arline says, "I know he'll be able to tell. I know I'm dead meat. I know I'm going to be fired."

Straight-faced, the floorman said, "I see nothing wrong with this drink, but I'll have the bartender make you a new one." He turned around to face Arline, and with his back to the players at the Baccarat table, he grimaced and silently mouthed, *Am I gonna die?*

\* \* \*

One day I come to work crying. "Del accused me of holding out on my tip income. I had a bad day yesterday, and he doesn't believe I made so little."

"Well, aren't you?" Dor asks.

It's 10:30 a.m. and we're in the dressing room getting ready for the day shift. Arline and the beautiful pale-skinned Korean girl, Mia, stop their conversation to listen.

In my innocence I look at Dor and whimper, "Aren't I what?"

Arline says, "Mia has six thousand dollars in her locker."

"Holding out," Dor says. "From your husband." At the same time she turns to Mia. "Jesus, Mia, what are you doing with six thousand dollars in your locker?"

"No," I mumble. "I give all my tips to my husband."

Arline rolls her eyes.

Mia, who is a former Miss Korea, stares at us like she's having trouble following the conversation. "I save money in my locker," she says.

Arline says to me, "What are you? Stupid? Everyone holds out."

I think Mia's the one who is stupid, keeping all that money in her locker. Dor and Arline make arrangements to take Mia and her money to a bank, and from that day on, I hold out from my new husband ten to fifteen dollars a day. I figure only God and I know how much money I make in tips—the IRS and Del get to guess.

* * *

The bartender I order my drinks from is good-looking in a jaded, dissipated way. Tommy's young, but his middle is on its way to the large belly of hard living. He has a biting wit, an ex-wife who works upstairs in accounting, a Stoli habit, and he snaps at me. Today I respond with tears, and I flee to hide out in the ladies' room. Dor is right behind me.

"I saw that!" she says. "I saw how he did that." She sits down next to me as I dab at my make-up and take a deep breath to compose myself. Part of me is angry at Tommy and part of me is embarrassed that I lost it at the bar.

"Listen to me," Dor continues. "I learned this from a cocktail waitress who took me under her wing at the Frontier and taught me to use my mouth as a weapon. Never—never—*never* let a bartender see you cry."

Her intensity has my attention. "Why?"

"You know Kim, the tall brunette in the Dice Pit? She was the head cocktail waitress at the Frontier, where I had my first job. She told me, 'This is what you do: when some man says something to you, you answer him in a way that he thinks you know everything. If that doesn't get his attention, then you tell him to go fuck himself.' Kim said, 'Believe me, before you know it, they'll all be treating you very nice, because they can't stand to be put down by a woman. Your mouth is your weapon. You don't need anything else, and they will never bother you.'"

Dor reaches across the counter and hands me another tissue. "Kim told me that, and you've heard *her* mouth. Besides, you know why Tommy's on you all the time."

I sniffle and shake my head. "No. I don't get it why he picks on me."

"He wants to fuck you."

My face must register my surprise, because Dor laughs. "Oh, yeah. And have you ever seen his ex-wife?" I shake my head again. "She comes down to the floor once in a while with paperwork for the pit clerks. You look just like her. That's why Tommy wants to fuck you."

I can't believe I didn't see this coming. Now it feels like being back in grade school, where the kids tell you that the boy who socked you in the arm did that because he likes you.

When we come out of the ladies' room, Lenny is sitting at the oyster bar. Luckily, he is so engrossed in chatting up Alice he hasn't noticed that Dor and I left our stations.

Dor's eyes narrow. "See that? I wondered why Lenny's eased up on hitting on me. I bet he's got Alice."

It is true that lately Alice has been selected more often to do pit breaks, where she can make a lot more money than in the Keno Lounge. When Lenny leaves the bar, Dor tries to talk to her.

"I didn't know you were dating Lenny," she says in a casual, could-care-less tone.

"Oh, we're not dating," Alice says. "We're just friends."

\* \* \*

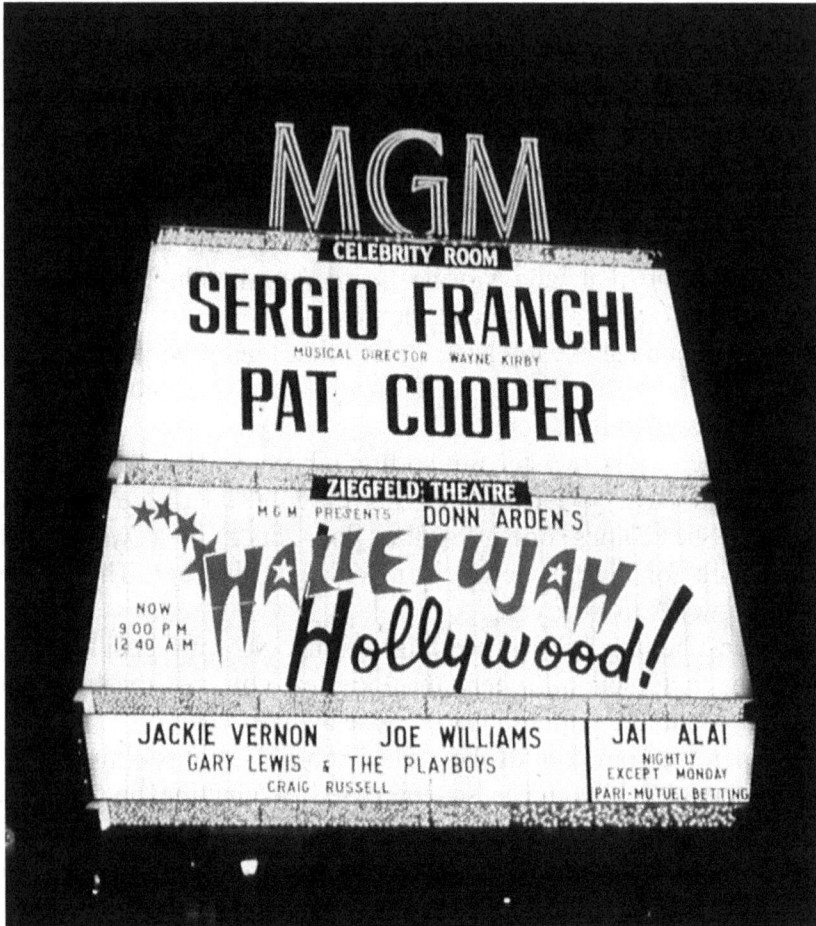

Comedian Pat Cooper headlines at the MGM

One afternoon I am serving drinks in the Keno Lounge when I'm approached by comedian Pat Cooper. He is currently appearing in the Celebrity Showroom with Italian-American singer Sergio Franchi.

He gets my attention and says, "Honey, see that lady over there?" He points to a nondescript woman slumped in one of the cushy red seats, studying several Keno tickets. "That's my wife."

He flips a red—a five dollar chip—onto my tray. "I'd really appreciate it if you'd bring her whatever she wants, as often as she wants."

I smile. "Of course. Thank you."

He smiles in return. "And do what you can to keep her here for the next two hours."

Two hours? Wonder what he is up to?

* * *

Isabella is a Cuban girl stationed in Pit One. She is lean, with dark, chocolate hair, honey-colored skin, maintains long red nails, and regularly comes to work dressed to the elegant nines because after 7 p.m. she has a hot date.

Arline's little sister Angie, who also worked Pit One, has been fired. She got outed when she called in sick to flounce off to Miami for four days with a high roller. Now Isabella only shares this lucrative station with one other waitress. The only girls doing better are Kim and the other girls who work in the Dice Pit, which is also called Craps.

Isabella is having a terrific day, getting blacks—one-hundred-dollar chips—from a New York player who has been there for several hours and is winning. The floormen are all over him, making sure he is happy. At the same time, they have changed out the dealer several times in an attempt to reverse the guy's luck.

Not everyone loves a winner.

Isabella has no idea of the shit storm ahead for her.

Arline has explained to me that, "Gambling is serious business. Serious gamblers are notoriously superstitious."

Some have their lucky charm, shirt, or girl friend. If a gambler loses a turn of the card or roll of the dice, he often takes it out on the dealer or the cocktail waitress. The poor dealer has to stand at the table, continue to deal the cards and take the guy's abuse.

"We cocktail waitresses are lucky," Arine says. "We can walk away."

Conversely, if the gambler thinks you've been lucky for him, he might toss onto your tray a big chip.

Mr. New York loves Isabella, and she knows how to play her part. He is smart enough to nurse his drinks, while he kibitzes and flirts with her to keep her nearby. Because of his attention, the floormen can't send her out of the pit, but they eye every move of this lucky dance.

At the end of the shift, Isabella has garnered from Mr. New York a considerable number of black chips, easily more than a thousand dollars. She is on her way to the escalator to go down to the dressing room when the casino manager intercepts her. She's "invited" into an office where there are two men in suits she doesn't know. They invite her to sit down.

Mr. New York "has a significant marker," they explain. A marker is a line of credit a player establishes in advance of the day he arrives. If he gambles his marker of say, $10,000, and his credit is good, he can ask for his marker—or credit limit—to be raised.

The suits tell Isabella that in essence this means, "the money he's been gambling with isn't his. It belongs to the casino." Isabella knows this is not true; the player has in fact taken a loan from the casino, which he is obligated to pay back. Whether he gambles that money, spends it on food, or tips or whatever, he still has to pay it back.

But by their reasoning the suits insist that the black chips Mr. New York has been giving her belong to the hotel. She cannot keep them. Please hand them over.

"It was so obvious they think cocktail waitresses are stupid," Isabella says. Her dark eyes glower in anger and frustration. "But what could I do?"

She succumbs to the shake-down. "They scared me. I managed to hide two chips in the dirty ashtrays, but I gave them the rest."

Arline nods and tucks a stray stand of blond hair between the top of one ear and the low side of her pillbox hat. "They resent the money we make," she says.

An idea occurs to me, and I say, "If they could figure out a way to eliminate tipping, I bet they would."

"How could they do that?" Ronni asks.

"Well, you know how they want gamblers to spend every dollar in their hotel. They could raise our wages, then establish a no-tipping policy in the casino. That would leave more money in the pockets of the players to gamble with."

Arline is horrified. "Never happen."

"Carolyn, I don't ever want to hear you say that again," Dor declares. "Don't give them any ideas."

## CHAPTER 13 – Warning notices

Louie Gumper, the swing shift bar manager, happens to be in the Reef Bar just before the end of my shift, and the next day I receive a pink warning notice he has written for chewing gum. In the corner of the top of the notice is my waitress number—46. I hate this number system.

At least in the Playboy Club we had identity. Every girl had a name, and if another girl had your name when you were hired, you had to choose another one. That was how I became Bunny Paige. Now I'm number 46—I feel like some kind of convict in red velour and a pillbox hat. I'm a number with cleavage.

Everyone knows Gumper does not see that well. He was on the other side of the Reef Bar, not in the service area standing next to me, and the numbers on those little red buttons are small. Since I never chew gum, I am incensed. I take three girls as witnesses with me to the bar manager's office to formally protest.

"You've *never* seen me chew gum," I tell Milton. "And no way could Louie Gumper read that number from so far away."

Milton does not admit out loud that Gumper probably could not see the number clearly, but he nods. In my determination to have this warning notice cancelled, I fall back on my mother's words when I was a kid. "Chewing gum in public makes you look cheap."

To my relief, the warning notice is rescinded.

* * *

Today Rhonda and Lily are having a contest to see how much bubble gum they can chew while they're working. At the service bar, Rhonda has just popped into her mouth her seventh wad of bubble gum.

Clap, clap. The floorman signals with his hands that she needs to come into the pit to take a drink order.

She picks up her tray and walks into the pit and says to the table of players, "Cocktails?" When she opens her mouth her sizable wad of gum falls out. It plops onto the blackjack table right next to the dealer's hand.

Timing is everything. At this moment, Milton walks by. He stops when he sees the ball of bright pink gum standing out against the green felt.

"Oh, *excuse* me," Rhonda says with her best smile. She hunches her shoulders even further and makes a show of delicately picking up the wad of gum with her manicured fingertips and pops it right back into her mouth. She chews and makes a big *crack*.

Milton glowers up at her face, as Rhonda is a good head taller than him. He says nothing and stomps off in the direction of the Dice Pit.

Rhonda does not care if she gets a warning notice for chewing gum, because she is satisfied that she has infuriated the assistant bar manager. To Rhonda and Lily it is a game to say outrageous things to Milton just to aggravate him. They know that they can harass the hell out of him and as long as they do not get two warning notices for the same action, union rules say they cannot be fired.

\* \* \*

Two hot chocolate orders lead to a friendly fight among the cocktail waitresses at the Reef Bar.

Betty prepares the two hot chocolates. Among other drink garnishes, there is always a can of whipped cream for coffee and hot chocolate drinks. Lily and Rhonda, bored, have hidden the can from Betty, our Mormon girl, in an attempt to get her confused. When Betty reaches for the can that is not there, Lily sprays a gob of whipped cream into her palm and flicks it at Betty's arm.

Betty flicks it back.

Rhonda grabs the can from Lily's hand and sprays whipped cream at Betty.

Meanwhile Betty has found another can pushed to the back of the shelf. She grabs it and sprays it in Rhonda and Lily's direction.

*Whoosht*, all over each other. Jayda, one of our black waitresses—at Playboy she'd be called a "chocolate" Bunny—arrives with a drink order just in time to get caught in cross-fire.

Whipped cream lands everywhere—on the drinks, on the trays, on the bar, on the bartender, on the girls' red hats and chests, and on a couple of men sitting near the end of the bar. Luckily the men are customers with a sense of humor. They watch this action with amusement.

At the height of the whipped cream fight, Milton appears.

"You girls will be the death of me!" he screams. "Clean this mess up now!"

The girls retire to the ladies room to clean themselves as best they can. Betty and Rhonda and Lily and Jayda get pink warning slips for "misuse of bar supplies."

* * *

In the first year that the MGM is open, Ronni racks up 26 of the pink things. She is the only waitress I know who gets a warning notice for not having her pillbox hat exactly one inch above her eyebrow.

At a quarter to seven—fifteen minutes before our day shift ends—Milton appears in the Reef Bar and says to Ronni, "They called and said they took your daughter to the hospital. They want you to go over there right away."

Ronni drops her tray, grabs her purse and flies out of the hotel. Later she tells me, "By the time I passed the dealers' room, I don't think I had any clothes on. I'd ripped off my uniform, and in the locker room, I just threw the uniform on the floor, grabbed my clothes, and put them on as I ran out of the hotel. Of course, I didn't sign out."

At the hospital Ronni is asked, "What took you so long? We called the hotel at two o'clock this afternoon!"

Pammy, Ronni's youngest daughter, is diabetic. The crisis is past, but Ronni is furious that Milton did not tell her until almost five hours after the hospital called.

During this time, Lenny calls the hospital to find out how Pammy is, probably to cover himself. Ronni has already gotten one warning notice for failure to sign out, and Lenny knows this. I imagine that in his head he was thinking that if he didn't tell her until it was almost time for her to get off, she'd run out without signing out and he could fire her.

Next day Ronni works her entire shift, burning inside, and saying nothing to anybody but me. At the end of the shift, she goes into the bar office to sign out. Milton is waiting. He hands her the pink warning notice and announces, "You're fired."

"I think he feels bad," she tells me later. "He doesn't like me, but I think it's just because he can't like me and stay on Lenny's good side."

This same night, Ronni takes her daughters to the MGM's gourmet Barrymore Room to join Arline and her kids to celebrate Angie's birthday. Angie and Ronni were in the same class at Vegas Valley High School.

They have just ordered their dinners when Danny Litwack enters the restaurant. Danny adores Ronni's two girls, whom he met when Ronni worked the front desk at Circus Circus. For her oldest daughter Courtney's birthday, he plans to comp dinner for Courtney and four of her friends for the Mack Davis show. Danny approaches the booth and says to Ronni, "Listen, I got your girls all set up. So, how you doin'? What's new?"

"I got fired," Ronni says.

Litwack's face tenses. "*What for?*" he booms.

Ronni tells him about Pammy's emergency and Lenny's actions. "Do you know that he didn't tell me for five hours that my daughter was in the hospital?"

The veins in Danny's neck pulse. Through tight teeth, he says, "Come with me." Ronni leaves her family and follows Danny to his office, where he calls Lenny Agnello at home.

"Listen," he says, "if Ronni is not on the floor tomorrow I'll have your job! I'll go to Benedict—I'll go to Kerkorian himself." Litwack's face takes on a purple hue. "*I'll have your fucking ass out the door.*"

Ronni, seeing this, worries that her friend is going to have a heart attack.

Litwack continues, seething into the phone. "How could you do this? You opened us up for a lawsuit. She could sue this hotel for what you did. For not telling her that her daughter was in the hospital."

Next morning Ronni enters the food and beverage office at 10:40 a.m. to sign in. She makes eye contact with Jane, Litwack's secretary. Jane is a clever cookie, young and pretty enough to decorate the bar office and old enough to know when to keep her mouth zipped. Lenny leans against his desk, puffing on his cigar.

"Why didn't you punch out yesterday?" he asks. "You know you're supposed to punch out. You know what the rules are."

Ronni forces herself to remain calm. She says, "Yes, I do know what the rules are. Nobody knows the rules better than I do." She looks Lenny right in the eye. "What is it? Why don't you like me? I do everything I'm supposed to. I never call in sick. I'm never late. I never complain. I come to work. I do what you want."

Lenny grunts and mumbles, "I run this department my way. I don't like people telling me where to put people."

A light of realization snaps on in Ronni's head. She says, "Did Danny ask you to put me in the pit?"

He does not directly answer her question. "Danny thinks he can tell me what to do," Lenny says, "but I run this department."

Ronni does not tell Lenny that she knows Danny put Angie in the pit and would have put her there, too, if she had asked. In fact, Ronni has bid for several pit shifts that became available since the hotel opened, and she has been passed over every time.

Instead she says, "I never asked Danny for anything. I tried to play by your rules. All I ask is to be treated like everybody else. If Danny asked you to put me in the pit, I'm sorry, but I never went to Danny. I never asked him for any special treatment."

The next day she calls Danny Litwack and cries, "Why did you do that? You caused me all these problems. Why? Why didn't you just leave me alone? If you hadn't gone to Lenny, I'd *be* in the pit by now."

She tells me Danny has promised her he will not say anything more to Lenny about putting her in the pit.

* * *

Dor has also gotten her share of pink warning slips. She is also careful never to get two for the same thing.

Lenny is seen less often on the floor now, and Milton has replaced him as the "stalker" whose job it is to police the floor and make sure the cocktail waitresses are doing their jobs without violating any bar department rules.

Dor laughs and jokes and tries to stay out of Milton's way. Her rule is: get in, serve the drinks, get out and mind your own business. I admire her perseverance. I don't know if I could maintain such calm on an extended basis if I knew so many people were out to get me.

Dor has begun to date a 21 dealer. Sometimes after work she goes into the dealers' room to chat with him. By the time she leaves the hotel, all the other day-shift cocktail waitresses are gone. One evening, it is 8:30 p.m. when she leaves the hotel. Walking to her car, she sees Lenny come out the door with Alice. Dor wonders what Alice is doing in the hotel so long after the end of the shift. Then it dawns on her that Alice was waiting for Lenny.

"This explains a lot," she says to me the next day. "Why Lenny is no longer hitting on me, why he doesn't even speak to me, and why Alice is getting pulled from the Keno Lounge every day to do pit breaks."

We are on our lunch break, sitting at a table in the Help's Hall with Kim and another girl from the Dice Pit. Kim asks, "So what are you going to do about it?"

Dor says, "Just what you taught me to do. Tell the truth, stick up for myself. No man's gonna push me around."

Kim says, "Well, I would've probably slept with him." Her smile erupts into laughter.

"You know I won't do that," Dor says.

"I know, but I'd have probably slept with the old bastard and got him off my back."

I am amused by all this delicious gossip. In silence I give thanks that I am not involved. I am just an observer.

Dor is not quiet about what she has seen. Alice no longer speaks to her. Four days later Dor finds she cannot open her locker. Someone has squirted superglue into it. A locksmith is called, and they have to take the lock out of the door and replace it.

## CHAPTER 14 – Vegas life, fun 'n gaming

Customers who gamble are not only given free drinks, but also free cigarettes. Cartons of just about every brand are kept in a cabinet in the center of Pit Two. One day Arline opens the cigarette drawer and sees a mouse.

"*Aaiiieeeee—*"

Her scream is punctuated by a *shwap* as she slams the drawer shut. She drops her tray. Glasses crash.

The happy life of an innocent mouse ends in a bloody squash between the back side of the drawer and the inside wall of the cabinet.

You have to wonder how a mouse gets into a big hotel casino, a casino the size of a football field. This cigarette cabinet is a long way from the nearest door, a long way from any kitchen.

None of the floormen will touch the drawer or the bloody mouse.

"What woosies," Lily says, adjusting her pink, heart-shaped glasses. From the Casino Bar we watch as security guards are called to remove the body of the dead mouse.

* * *

No grand hotel complex would be complete without a house doctor. Have a sniffle? Need an aspirin? Feet swollen? Cocktail waitresses can go downstairs to the office of our own Dr. Tippet any time, for any malaise, no charge. Dr. Tippet is a partner with Dr. Elias Ghanem—famous for being Elvis' personal Vegas physician—in the Las Vegas Medical Centers.

However, nothing is "free."

You have to listen through Dr. Tippet's lengthy, serious and unusual diagnosis of your malaise, and his standard advice: what you need is a boob job, and he is just the doctor to do it.

I am disgusted to hear this, and I make a mental note that no matter how sick I might feel one day, I will never go downstairs to the hotel doctor.

* * *

Bartender Tommy's focus on me escalates to straightforward harassment. "When are we going to fuck?" he asks.

I follow Dor's advice: treat it as a joke and make a smartass answer. "I'd screw you in California, but I can't in Vegas 'cause I'm Lutheran."

Tommy's look tells me he is trying to figure out what I just said. Meanwhile I pick up my tray and depart from the service bar area.

* * *

In such a large public area like a casino, with so many people coming and going, it is not uncommon for personal items to be placed on a bar, chair or gaming table and then be forgotten when the player leaves.

On a vacant chair in the Keno Lounge, I find a prescription bottle of little white pills. I continue to pick up dirty glasses and take drink orders from Keno players and head back to the service bar. I set my tray on the bar and give Tommy my order and say, "Look what I found in the Lounge. Somebody's meds. They might be looking for it."

Tommy picks up the bottle, flips off the cap, rattles the pills, and upends the bottle into his mouth. I watch, dumbfounded, as he takes a hefty swallow from the glass of vodka he keeps handy and says, "Well, let's see which way they go—up or down."

On the green felt of a 21 table a player leaves behind a pack of Marlboro cigarettes. Arline arrives at the bar with the pack on her tray, lifts the lid and discovers, nestled among the Marlboros, a large, well-wrapped joint of marijuana. She replaces the lid and slips the pack of cigarettes with its little surprise into her purse on the shelf below the bar.

When a tiny vial of cocaine is left behind on a table in Pit One, the floorman calls two security guards. The guards take the vial away. Dor asks Milton what the guards will do with it, and he says,

"It wasn't coke, if that's what you're thinking. You girls have too much imagination."

I interpret this to mean he doesn't know.

\* \* \*

Arline attracts her share of critters. She is just getting over the stress of the mouse-in-the-cigarette-drawer incident when she serves a players' drink and a three-inch, flying black cockroach—locals call them "water bugs"—falls from the cupid-painted ceiling onto the green felt of the 21 table.

Its arrival scatters drinks and cards and players.

\* \* \*

Pit Two floorman Jerry Russell is young, cute, and has a pregnant wife. This does not prevent him from tormenting cocktail waitresses.

I cannot imagine anything more boring than being a floorman in a blackjack pit. Yes, they dress well, in suits always meticulously coordinated with shirt and tie. Their job is to watch the games, look out for cheating—by players or by dealers—note who is winning and who is losing, be sure no Gaming Control Board rules are broken, hand out comps to players, answer their questions and keep them happy. Floormen may also set the dealers' work schedules.

In the hierarchy of gaming, floormen are middle managers who answer to the pit boss and the casino manager. They stand in a limited area for eight hours.

Jerry's favorite joke is to stick out his tongue and talk about how good he is, how he has a "black belt in Tongue Fu."

Arline says, "He's probably compensating because he's hung like a stud gerbil."

Today is Jerry's birthday. Arline presents him with a shoebox-sized gift, wrapped in pretty tissue and ribbon. "A little present from all the girls," she says with her sweetest smile.

Right in the middle of the pit he opens the box. When he lifts the lid, his face crimsons. Inside is the result of Arline's early morning trip to the butcher: a raw cow's tongue.

* * *

When you are young and pretty and dressed to impress, you can go anywhere in Vegas and never pay for anything. For MGM cocktail waitresses, everything is comped.

"Please come into the lounge and have a drink."

"Would you like to have dinner in our gourmet room?"

"Would you like to see Tom Jones' show?"

"Would you like to meet The Checkmates?"

It is like being a high roller, but with no gambling obligation. All we are expected to do is dress up, show some cleavage, and tip, which we do, and quite well.

We do not pay any attention to which chips we have in our purses—supermarkets, dry cleaners, local businesses and all casinos accept any casino's chips in lieu of cash. I always seem to have a lot of money in my purse. When I think about it, it seems bizarre. Before I moved to Vegas, the most I usually carried in my purse at one time was $20. Now I regularly carry two or three hundred.

One night Lara, Ronni, Dor, Lily and I casino-hop, visiting seven Strip hotels before our evening ends. It only takes us about ten minutes to leave one casino, drive to the next, valet park in the porte-cochère, and enter. Each of the girls knows a floorman, pit boss or executive in one of the casinos, and that person knows we are MGM Grand cocktail waitresses. We are treated like queens. We are not expected to gamble. We decorate the casino. Everywhere we appear, our glamorous presence is good for business.

I can see why some people refer to Las Vegas as "Disneyland for adults."

* * *

Business at the MGM has stabilized. The newness of the biggest casino in town has worn off. Most of the gaming action takes place on the swing shift, so during the day we have downtime. Some days it is a challenge to stave off boredom.

We invent a game called, "Guess which cocktail waitress—?"

Guess which cocktail waitress went to Woodstock? There, in the back of a van, Diane gave birth to her son.

Guess which cocktail waitress was an English teacher in an all-girls school in Pasadena, California? Haley, who works in the Parisian Bar.

Guess which cocktail waitress is a Mormon girl from Utah? Betty, of course, who was surprised to discover that roasted pig tastes like pork.

Guess which cocktail waitresses are former Playboy Bunnies? I was a Bunny in Detroit and Kim was a Bunny in San Francisco.

Another day Ronni and I write naughty limericks about all the girls. Not all of our limericks are flattering. We do not spare ourselves, either.

Ronni writes:
*"My friend Carolyn lives for pleasure,*
*fucking and sucking at her leisure.*
*But for her a real treat is something to eat.*
*Her love of good food's beyond measure."*

* * *

A love/hate relationship exists between casino workers and tourists. When business is slow, everyone becomes anxious because it means we make less money. When it is busy, everyone complains that there are more nut cases gambling. A full moon, it is said, *really* brings out the worst in players. In some of the cheap gift shops in town, you can buy a tee shirt that says, "I'm not a tourist—I live here."

I resist the temptation to buy the one that says, "Eat, drink, and be merry, for tomorrow you may be in Utah."

Putting on the tourist/customers in the MGM is an ongoing game. We cannot help ourselves. Some of the questions they ask seem so ignorant. Tourists only see the casinos, never Las Vegas' residential neighborhoods. Visitors from the east coast think we commute to work from Los Angeles. Others think we live in the hotels.

A player asks Ronni, "Say, how do you get a job like this?"

"Oh, here it was easy," she replies. "We only had to blow the top four bosses."

When some guy tells me I am beautiful, I have learned to smile and say, "Not bad for a guy in drag, huh?"

The scary part is that men believe this stuff.

One afternoon Ronni, Lara and I are standing in front of a bank of slot machines near the Baccarat pit, gossiping. Two couples approach. One woman says to her husband, "I'm telling you, it's in this hotel. Here, we'll ask these girls."

She approaches Lara and says, "There's a famous pancake restaurant here, but I don't know the name of it. Can you tell us where it is?"

Without batting a mascaraed eyelash, Lara says, "Oh sure, down that way—"she points towards the jai alai courts—"and you go just past the coffee shop. It's in the back of the next restaurant."

As the two couples head towards the coffee shop, the wife says to her husband, "See, I told you they would know."

Ronni and I look at Lara. "What pancake restaurant?" I ask.

Ronni says, "I never heard anything about a pancake restaurant."

Lara giggles. "Oh, I made that up. But see, that's what they wanted to hear. They went away happy, didn't they?"

* * *

You cannot work in a place like the MGM in Las Vegas and wear a skimpy costume and think no one you—or your parents—know is ever going to see you.

One day I am offering free drinks in the Keno Lounge and staring up at me in the second row is the entire family of a girl I was on a Jobs Daughters' drill team with in high school. Her father, two Keno tickets in each hand, is a high mucky-muck Shriner.

"Carolyn!" They exclaim. "What are you doing here?"

See what I mean about dumb tourist questions? Isn't it obvious I'm working here?

I have a good job making a lot of money, so why are my cheeks flushing? It is not as if they are going back to Seattle to tell my parents, who already know, anyway. When I became a Playboy Bunny, my parents kept it a secret from friends and family, but now they are resigned to my strange job choices.

The members of the Smith family recover well from their surprise and chat with me cordially. Still, I feel embarrassed, like I should have a more respectable job. I muse on the fact that only in Las Vegas are showgirl, dealer, and cocktail waitress jobs considered to be highly desirable and respectable.

One day I am working the pits as the break girl and am hailed by a little Jewish woman playing blackjack.

I recognize her as the mother of a lawyer I used to date in Los Angeles. Stephen brought me to Vegas once for a weekend. He said his father was a member of the Jewish mafia. I had never heard of a Jewish mafia, and I thought he was simply trying to impress me.

I was the only girl Stephen took home to the Bronx to meet his parents. I flash on the memory. He hadn't left enough driving time from Washington DC for me to change my clothes, and he hadn't told me it was the Jewish Passover seder dinner. I walked braless into a house full of relatives who engulfed me with the question, "Do you like children?"

Now Stephen's mother calls to her husband playing at the next table, "Maury, Maury, look!" She points at me. "It's the girl who got away!"

\* \* \*

When Lenny is not following Alice, he is following Lara. When he opens his mouth to speak, his words are preceded by a stream of cigar smoke. "When are you gonna give me some of that?" he says, staring at Lara's tits.

Lara makes a high-pitched, embarrassed giggle. "Listen, it's so bad the only reason guys come back twice is, they can't believe it was that bad the first time. It wouldn't be any good."

"Believe me," Lenny jokes, "I'd make it good."

Lara is disgusted by this exchange, which happens more than once. "What a son of a bitch," she tells us. "I couldn't fuck him with someone else's prick, you know what I'm saying?"

I wash the image of a naked Lenny Agnello in a bed clouded by cigar smoke right out of my mind. Lara is right, it is disgusting.

But it is part of the environment in which we work. And it is not so disgusting that any girl would think of quitting on the basis of some women's lib issue. We make too much money.

* * *

The man lies on his back on the red, lion-logo-spotted carpet at the edge of Pit Three, his eyes closed, his face pale. One hand clutches the leg of the stool from which he has fallen, as if to let go would mean he would lose his chance of beating the house's hand as soon as he rises from the dead.

Spread around him is a myriad of lifesaving equipment. Paramedics, faces as serious as any high roller with a kingdom at stake, focus on what they can do to save the man's life.

This scene greets me when I arrive on the floor at 11 a.m. Today I have been pulled out of the Keno Lounge to work the 21 pit and this is what I get.

Watching the action with his usual lack of expression is the floorman, Dixson. He wears his usual color-coordinated shirt, custom-tailored suit, silk tie and tinted glasses. He glances at his gold watch. No doubt he is wondering how much longer this life-saving will take before he can reopen the pit.

Only the table from which the man collapsed has remained open. This is a five-dollar minimum 21 table. Moments ago there had been two men sitting next to each other. Now there is only one. He sits slumped on his high padded chair betting heavily, stacks of red ($5), green ($25) and black ($100) chips between his open hands. A blank-faced dealer lays cards in front of him with hands that do not even shake. Neither seems mindful of the drama playing out at their feet.

How can they act like nothing out of the ordinary is happening? How can a man gamble when the guy next to him just fell off his stool and could be dead? The only things missing from this surreal scene are movie cameras.

"Stay away from here," Dixson growls when he sees me. "Get me a scotch on the rocks, and then wait at the bar."

I deliver his scotch as instructed, return to the Reef service bar, and pour myself a cup of coffee. There won't be anything for me to do until the body is removed—alive or dead—and the paramedics and all their equipment leave the pit.

* * *

Two days a week Lara and Arline work together doing pit breaks. Arline begins to date Joey, a dealer in Pit Two, and is paranoid someone might tell him how old she is. Not that she has revealed her age, but she is afraid one of the girls will point out to him that she is "older." She gives the waitress she breaks in Pit Two a little longer time, so she can linger in the presence of the object of her affection.

Arline gets some diet pills from her doctor, and shares them with Lara. Pink and white, they are called Didrex.

"They're just nice," Lara says. "They don't make you too nervous."

Lara and Arline like the pills because they think when they take them, they can work harder, move faster, hustle more drinks. They are wired like cheap toasters.

After work, they decide to go have a drink together.

"Village Pub?" Lara asks.

This is the regular after-work hangout for MGM day shift dealers and cocktail waitresses because it is conveniently located on Koval Lane, just behind the MGM. Land developer and realtor Frank Ellis built the Pub in 1968 with typical Vegas interior design: maroon leather booths, dark wood beamed ceiling and tables, red walls, fireplace in the lounge, beer and ale on draft. The prints on the walls are supposed to authenticate that old-English pub feeling. The place is open twenty-four hours, so I imagine it is as popular with swing and graveyard as it is with our day shift.

"Nah, I don't want to run into Joey tonight. And no hotel where we don't know somebody," Arline says. "Otherwise, they'll think we're hookers."

Lara brightens. "I know just the place," she says. "Le Café. Paradise and Trop. Only fags go there. They'll think we're lesbians, so no one will bother us."

When Lara and Arline report that Le Café turns out to be a safe place to get soused, it becomes popular with all the girls.

* * *

Discotheques come and go in Las Vegas: the first one, chrome and mirrored JB's, opened in 1973. It was followed by Dirty Sally's and Billy Jack's.

Lara likes Billy Jack's. "They've got Larry Taylor, the cutest deejay."

"You just like him because he has hair," Arline says. "You like 'em hairy."

Lara giggles. It is true that Larry Taylor has long bangs, thick shoulder-length curls, and an elaborate mustache.

Tonight Lara, Ronni, Arline and I have dinner at the newly-opened Italian family restaurant, The Bootlegger, on Eastern Avenue. Owners Blackie Hunt and Lauri Perry are former Las Vegas lounge entertainers, so they know how to schmooz their customers. This is how I would imagine you would be treated if you were mafia princesses.

Over coffee and Amaretto, a new almond-flavored liqueur I have just discovered, Ronni says, "Let's hit Snoopies! I wanna see how they changed it."

Snoopies disco is the former Yellow Submarine, on the strip between the Sands Hotel and Flamingo Road. It is midnight when we arrive. The dance floor is full, the beat is steady, and the mirrored, rotating, overhead ball shoots colored lights into every dark corner. At the bar there is standing room only. What else would you expect on a Thursday night in Las Vegas?

I am snaking around on the dance floor when some guy I don't know snaps a popper under my nose. I can't help but inhale. The amil nitrate, a popular sexual excitant, races straight to my brain.

In my vision, the edges of the dance floor tilt in opposite directions. The world is truly flat, not round. I bump past two other dancers, stagger to a chair, and almost knock it over in my attempt to sit. I am dizzy and my heart races like I have just run a marathon. I am *mad*.

Ronni sees me and yells over the amplified music, "Are you okay?"

"No!" I shout. "Some asshole just popped an ami on me."

She gets me a glass of water. I drink it, and shake my head. The room tilts again. "You guys have fun. I'm just going to sit here for a while." I am afraid to move.

It takes an hour—during which I do not drink any alcohol—before my racing heartbeat slows, and I feel halfway normal.

After that experience, the gay Le Café becomes our favorite dance place. The attraction for the cocktail waitresses is that we don't need a partner to dance with, we can dance with each other, no macho guys hit on us, and the chance of being assaulted by some guy trying to drug us, is lessened.

One night we run into one of our bartenders, Larry. He is friendly, we all have a few drinks, and toward dawn everybody goes home. The next day we see Larry at work and tell him what fun we had with him the night before. He says, "Oh, that wasn't me, that was my twin brother, Gary."

Why is he saying this? Does he think we'll think he is gay because we ran into him at Le Café? What's the big deal? Larry has *heterachromia iridis*: the condition of having one brown eye and one blue eye. It occurs in approximately one in every thousand people. Not likely that he has a twin.

Now Larry thinks that because we had a few drinks with him, he will get lucky and one of us will fuck him. Toward that end, he brings to work Polaroid pictures of his genitalia, which he refers to as "Big Jim and the Twins."

Guaranteed to turn a girl off.

* * *

I still do a little free-lance graphic design work for Joy Hamman, who just landed as a client the recently-built Regency Towers.

Overlooking the greenery of the Las Vegas Country Club's eighteen-hole golf course, Regency Towers is the first luxury condominium highrise in Las Vegas. She is also pitching the next-scheduled highrise, the Jockey Club condominiums. Sitting on ten acres, the Jockey Club will have two eleven-story towers and will overlook the Dunes' Emerald Green Golf Course. She hires me to do spec ads for both projects.

Word gets around the casino that I am an artist. I begin to get commissions to paint portraits in oil. I paint a mural in acrylics in the stairwell wall of Diane's new condo across from the university.

One of the waitresses who works in slots, Mariella, a single mom with two kids, says she paints in oils, too. She would like me to come to her apartment some time and see her work, but we never seem to be able to agree on a time.

Mariella appears to always have a date, and she favors men of community importance. One day she comes to work with an amusing story about attending a party over the weekend where Clark County District Attorney Roy Woofter was so drunk he entertained everyone by crawling under the coffee table, pretending to be a dog, and barking, "Woof, woof, woof."

I wonder if Del's friend Jeff, who works in District Attorney Woofter's office, was at the party.

Mariella's latest romantic interest is Nevada's new Lieutenant Governor, Bob Rose. She confides that on her day off they met for lunch and in his car in the parking garage of the Federal Building she gave him a blow job.

## CHAPTER 15 – How to screw your best friend

Cocktail waitresses think dealers make more money. Dealers think cocktail waitresses make more money. Bartenders think everybody else makes more money. I never met so many jealous, discontented people who hate their jobs.

Susan, who works with Kim in the Dice Pit, quits. She and her boyfriend have made plans to sail to Hawaii.

"Oh, it's so romantic," gushes Fran, the third Dice-Pit waitress. Fran is a petite blonde with a Marilyn Monroe voice. Fran carries a huge tote bag to work every day that usually holds four or five romance novels. She's a big fan of historical romance author Kathleen Woodiwiss, and is currently reading *The Wolf and the Dove*. Her locker is stuffed with more romance novels, and I wonder if this is because Fran's husband won't let her read them at home.

A few weeks later word comes back about Susan and her boyfriend. Their sailboat broke a rudder in a violent storm and they drifted in the ocean for four terrifying days before being found and rescued.

"See what happens when you think you can do something else?" says Fran, "that's what she gets for thinking she's better than the rest of us."

This kind of thinking—and a terrific income—keeps people from changing jobs, from doing anything to better their unhappy lives.

Yet Susan's departure is an unspoken welcome event—it presents a chance for someone else to increase her income by getting a better shift position. And the Dice Pit is the plum station. Everyone wants to be there.

Thanks to the culinary union, there are rules of seniority regarding who can be awarded open shift positions. A girl can only bid on an available position once every three months, so—just like gambling—you have to calculate your timing. If I bid on this position and don't get it, and someone else with a desirable position quits next week, I won't be eligible to bid on her position. So, do I jump now? Or wait to see if there's something else coming? In the world of casino cocktail waitressing, there's a hierarchy based on how much money a certain shift and position can make.

Even children are aware of this. At a birthday party for one of the girls I once heard, "My mommy works in the pit, and your mommy only works in slots."

Every girl who opened the hotel and hasn't yet gotten a pit assignment lies in wait for a pit waitress to quit or get fired so they can bid for her job. By the summer of 1974, the only original hires who haven't quit or made it to the pit are Ronni, Dor and I.

Alice has bid for and gotten a permanent pit assignment. Ronni and Dor and I have applied for every available pit shift and been passed over every time.

Dor is resigned. She says, "Lenny hates me. He won't pick me till I'm the last girl left with opening seniority, and the union will force him."

At home I share Susan's harrowing sailing story with Del. "That's great news!" he exclaims, "I'll wire it up through Paul so you can get her job."

I drop my dishtowel in surprise. "What?"

Del sees a terrific opportunity. "Morrie Jaeger's a good friend of Paul's. All I have to do is make a phone call, and it's a done deal. You're juiced in."

I've seen Morrie Jaeger around the casino. With his slick dark hair, fat dark eyebrows and quiet demeanor, the casino manager makes me think of a robotic watchdog. Just looking at him intimidates me.

I think about what Del says. Something doesn't feel right. My best casino girlfriend and I are eligible and one of us is likely to be picked for the tasty Dice Pit job. If we all bid, we know Lenny won't choose Dor. I can use my juice and ace Ronni out. A voice in my head—probably my mother's—says, "You weren't raised to behave this way. You weren't raised to *screw*—my word, not my mother's—your best friend."

Yeah, but I can. And there's a lot of money on the line here.

Mom's voice says, "Just because you can, doesn't mean you should."

Del thinks I should. "All's fair in love, war and cocktails," he says. He doesn't see any moral conflict here.

I agree to sleep on it. The next morning I wake up disgusted with myself that I even considered using my juice to take this job away from Ronni. While I've made money in the Keno Lounge, Ronni has worked her butt off and nearly starved to death in the Reef Lounge schlepping those oysters to low-tipping cash customers.

Okay, her husband has a good job as a Maitre d' in the Aladdin showroom, but they also have two kids. The least I must do is enter this contest fairly.

But I choose a different direction.

I tell Del, "I can't do it. Not a word to Paul. I'm not signing up for the Dice Pit. I'll sign for the next pit opening."

Ronni and Dor sign the bid sheet, and Ronni gets Susan's job.

## CHAPTER 16 – Keeping up the PC

Three days a week Lenny makes Dor do bar breaks—a low-tip job—and on my days off he lets her work the Keno Lounge. "He's trying to get me to quit," she says.

With Ronni now working in the Dice Pit, the Reef Lounge station is open. Not even slot waitresses want it, but Lenny doesn't post the opening. Instead he informs me that I will work both the Keno Lounge and the Reef Lounge. Having a single waitress work both a free-drink position and a cash-bar position is unheard of—it opens the door for big-time opportunities to steal from the hotel. Lenny doesn't seem concerned about this.

I am not happy to be placed in this situation, but I can't object without the risk of bringing Lenny's brand of harassment down on my own head.

For one thing, it means I now have to bring a two-hundred-dollar bank to work with me every day to pay for the damned shrimp and oysters and Reef Lounge drinks. When I return to the Keno Lounge after serving customers in the Reef, the Keno players now greet me with "Finally", and "Jesus, bring me a drink!" and "Where the hell have you *been*?" If it's a busy day, both locations greet me with hostility. Not fun.

In my worst Fellini nightmare, *Muriel Rothkopf, wife of executive vice-president Bernie Rothkopf, arrives in the Reef with her girlfriends to enjoy their usual orgy of oysters and shrimp. She sees no waitress in sight, and is made to wait a conspicuously long time to be served. She goes home and complains to her husband. Bernie goes to Lenny and says, "Where the hell was the Reef waitress?" What's in it for Lenny to tell the truth? He gives me a warning notice for "leaving my station." Not happy with this, Bernie presses because his wife had to wait, and I get fired.*

God, what a nightmare scenario.

\* \* \*

Because of having to cover two stations at the same time, my daily tip income declines dramatically. Lenny's next move is to limit the number of drinks allowed to be served per shift in the Keno Lounge. Tommy must keep a tally of every alcoholic beverage I serve there—no limit on soft drinks.

My challenge now is to calculate which players deserve the free alcoholic drinks.

If I have a big tipper in the lounge, I have to make sure I have enough drinks left to keep him happy. If a big tipper shows up an hour before my shift ends, and I've served my alcoholic limit, I'm screwed. He doesn't get a drink because I'm hiding from the Keno customers in the break room behind the Keno writers. I only emerge at 7 p.m. when the swing shift girl relieves me. I take my last catcalls and insults for the day as I pass through the lounge to the bar to get my purse and leave.

I have been instructed by both Lenny and Milton that I am not to discuss this new free-drink limit thing with customers.

It occurs to me that there are some drinks that don't need a full shot of booze. If I have an order for both a scotch and water and a scotch and tonic, for instance, I can order the water and tonic on the side and only one shot of scotch. By mixing the drinks myself on the way to the Keno Lounge, I've served two alcoholic drinks for the "price" of one.

If a player complains that the drink doesn't taste very strong, I give him a flip remark and what I hope is my sexiest smile. Or I give him a sad smile, play helpless waitress, and blame it on the bartender.

In a pinch, I encourage the player to complain to management, but I beg him not to say I suggested it. I cozy up to him like we're both conspirators in this together, and I just know he'll keep my secret.

If anybody ever does complain to management, I never hear about it, and nothing changes. What does the hotel care? They're making money hand over greedy fist.

It's all about the business of liquor expense. About "keeping the PC up." What is the PC? I've never heard of this before, but Dor understands how it works.

PC stands for the percentage. She says, "Let's say that we started out a brand new hotel, and at the end of the month we have to have a PC count to find out how much liquor is being sold, to find out if anyone's stealing. Let's say by the end of the month there are seven shots left in a bottle, so we've sold X number of shots out of that bottle. You consider how much should have been charged for it, compared to how much was taken in. If it's pretty close, you're okay. If the PC—the percentage—is way off, somebody's either drinking or stealing."

We're standing at the service bar on an easy day, killing time. Tommy says, "You girls looking for something to do this evening?"

"Fuck off," Dor says, "I'm teaching her about the PC and stealing. Go have another drink."

"So what does it mean when they say the PC is up or down?" I ask.

"If it's *up*, that means the shots poured and money amounts are close enough to even. If it's *down*, that means not enough money was taken in to match the shots poured. So, either somebody's giving drinks away or they're selling drinks and pocketing the money or they're drinking."

I begin to understand that every drink poured must be accounted for, either with cash paid, or a player freebie. The latter is counted and "charged" against the budgets for different areas, such as Keno, or Pit Three. I don't know why, but Lenny is using "We have to keep the PC up" as an excuse to limit the drinks in the Keno Lounge.

"What's he thinking?" I ask Dor.

"What they're trying to do is take drinks allotted for Keno and give them away in 21. Keep the 21 players happy because their bets are bigger than the players in Keno."

"Is there a limit to the amount of comps they can give away?"

"No, it's all a write-off."

I'm really confused. "Then why would they put a limit in Keno?"

"Because of the stealing. Somebody's stealing out the back door, taking cases of liquor. Now let's say they assigned X number of cases to the Reef Bar, and now there's a case short. Well, what happened to it? Must have given it away in comps. All of a sudden you've got a lot on comps, for what? They log it next to how much money was spent in Keno. Does it come out of there? They didn't have that much business in Keno, but we went through this and this and this. Does it tally out? Now where did the cases go? So you end up looking like a drunk or an asshole: Carolyn drinks, or she gave away all these drinks trying to make money for herself. They've got to make somebody look like a scapegoat."

"And only I would know."

"Now if they ever listened to Carolyn, they'd figure out what was going on, but who listens to a cocktail waitress? All they think is that you wanted to hustle, hustle, hustle to make more money. That's what they think cocktail waitresses want to do. So here you're hired to do a job, and you're standing there all day, and people are bugging you for drinks and you're at your limit. What do you tell people?"

Tommy, who's been listening to this exchange, says, "Inch by inch, life's a cinch, yard by yard, life's a bitch."

I get more creative with my drink scam. I leave the vodka completely out of Bloody Marys, so it counts only as a plain tomato juice. I figure with enough hot sauce in the tomato juice and the right lime garnish, the player won't miss the taste of vodka. I squirt heavy on the Worcestershire and Tabasco.

One day Lenny happens to be at the bar when I'm doing this. I've gotten so cavalier about my no-alcohol drink scam that I don't notice he's watching.

"Jesus Christ!" Lenny says. "You put enough hot sauce in there to kill the son of a bitch!"

Big-mouth Betty, standing next to me says, "That's so they won't miss the vodka."

I freeze in place, well aware that this can get me fired. I can't imagine how Lenny would phrase this on the warning notice, but I know it wouldn't be nice.

To my amazement, he harrumphs on his cigar and walks away from the bar. The whole meaning has gone right over his head. This time, I am grateful for his stupidity.

* * *

The next two days are my days off. When I return to work on Thursday—my "Monday"—I learn that yesterday in the Keno Lounge Dor was attacked.

When she comes to break the Reef Lounge, I ask, "What happened?"

She laughs. "A guy grabbed my leg as I was passing through there. I said, 'I'm sorry, but I'm past my limit.'"

"Jeez, you're not supposed to say anything about the limit."

"Well, I do. I won't lie for Lenny or anybody. The players get angry. Who gives a shit about your limit? They don't understand what that means. They're gambling, and they want their free drinks."

"What did you do?"

"He jerked me around, I lost my balance, and all the glasses flew all over the place. He was furious. Can you believe it? He was going to beat me up because I wouldn't bring him a drink. About fifteen times when he asked, I told him I'd be right back. I tried to explain to him there was nothing I could do about it. I tried to cover my ass, but it didn't do any good."

"What did Lenny say?"

"He doesn't give a shit. I hid out the rest of the shift. You shoulda been here. You missed all the fun."

## CHAPTER 17 – Math, war & cocktails

It's fall, known for Back-to-School, Halloween, Thanksgiving and the end of daylight savings time.

Spring forward, fall backward.

On the day before we turn our clocks back, I arrive at the hotel, I dress, I go to the bar office to sign in for my shift. Four other girls are signing in at the same time. Lenny stands in his doorway, puffing on a new cigar, watching us. Makes me wonder, does he get hot watching cocktail waitresses sign in? More likely, he's watching for one of us to do something wrong so he can write yet another warning slip. Doesn't he have anything better to do?

On the wall above the sign-in clipboard, there's a notice hand-printed in big block letters announcing the change this evening back from daylight savings time.

Lenny says, "Don't you forget to change your clocks back tonight." Puff, puff. "I don't want to hear you forgot to set your clock back." Puff, puff. "Anybody who's late to work tomorrow because they forgot to set their clock back will be fired. If one of you girls is late, you get fired, no excuses."

Math isn't my best subject, but what he's saying makes no sense. If you *don't* set your clock back tonight, you'll be an hour *early* for work tomorrow. I think, this guy doesn't need a full moon to be nuts.

I can't help myself. "But Lenny, if we don't turn back our clocks," I say, "we'll be an hour *early*, not late."

Ronni jabs me in the side. The girls make loud, shushing noises. Never one to know when to keep my mouth shut, I turn to the girls and continue, "But it's true, you can't possibly be late if you forget to set your clock back."

Everyone turns to look at Lenny. His scowl is so dark, it's mesmerizing. He takes his cigar out of his mouth, turns around, enters his office and slams the door.

\* \* \*

Lenny continues giving Dor warning notices. It seems like any time you see Dor, you expect to see Milton right behind her.

Then she gets another warning notice: her heels are too high, her hat is too low, her hair is too long, she was late returning from a break, she was standing too far away from her station. Honestly, you'd think these guys get their rocks off by giving warning notices. Dor takes it all with amazing resilience.

Lenny has called her into his office one more time and propositioned her. "This is your last chance," he tells her.

She's laughed it off, saying to him, "Lenny, I can't do that."

She tells me he said, "Well, it doesn't seem to be a problem for other people."

"What did he mean by that?" I wonder out loud.

"I have no idea," she says, "but I'd bet somebody's sleeping with him."

Now it appears that for some reason Lenny really hates Dor. His next move is to try to get her for stealing. He turns her in to the IRS. They respond amazingly fast with a tax audit, but Dor has kept good tip records.

"The way girls mess up, you know?" she says, "If you work the Cub Bar, and you don't keep track of those tips you get on the checks, and you put down some phony thing, they nail you." She passes the audit.

She says Lenny has threatened her. He has told her, "You'll never work in the 21 pit."

With this kind of pressure on her, I'm not surprised when Dor gets sick. She asks to go home, and Lenny says, no. Turns out her doctor thought she had an ulcer but she's diabetic. She has had a bunch of tests and found out she's been taking ulcer medicine that shouldn't be taken when you're a diabetic.

At the Casino Bar she collapses. Ronni feels a tray shoved into her back and hears Dor whisper, "Grab my tray," before she passes out. Arline, behind Dor, tries to break her fall, but Dor hits her head on a slot machine. Security comes with oxygen, and puts damp cloths on her forehead.

Someone must have called the bar department, because not three minutes have gone by before Lenny and his cigar appear. He stands over Dor's limp body lying on the carpet and stares at her.

One of the security guards asks, "Should we call an ambulance?"

Lenny puffs. "I don't care what you do. I don't care if the bitch dies." He walks away.

Ronni says, "What a terrible, cruel, cold thing to say!"

"The man is sick," Arline declares.

Alice says, "Oh, I'm sure he didn't really mean it."

We look at Alice like she's gone over to the enemy side.

Just then Dor comes to. Security has called the paramedics, who arrive with a gurney. One of the paramedics asks her, "Are you pregnant?"

"No, I'm okay." With help, Dor sits up.

The paramedics want to take her out of the hotel on the gurney, just to be safe.

Lenny, who didn't go far, steps right back into the situation. He says, "She can't take the uniform out of the building."

The paramedic is young, kind of a good-looking guy. His expression registers his astonishment. He stares at Lenny's cigar and says, "What do you want to do, take all her clothes off right here? She has to go *now*, to the hospital."

Lenny: "She can't leave the premises with hotel property."

Paramedic: "She's going to the hospital."

Puff puff. Lenny backs down.

They help Dor lean and roll onto the gurney and they carry her downstairs to the bar office. Litwack is away from the property, and when they arrive his secretary, Jane, already has the door open.

Inside they help Dor move from the gurney into a wheelchair. Breathing cigar smoke into everyone's faces, Lenny watches all this with open disapproval. Puff puff puff.

Jane explains to Lenny that with everyone involved—meaning lots of witnesses—it's best to let Dor go to the hospital right away, in her uniform. She says to Lenny, "I'm sure you understand that this is what Mr. Litwack would want." Jane is very diplomatic.

Lenny can say no more. He twitches and fumes and puffs as the paramedics wheel Dor in her red uniform, hat askew, out of the hotel.

\* \* \*

Tommy continues to pressure me to have sex with him. His standard come-on line is, "Carolyn, when are we gonna fuck?" The fact that I'm married means nothing to him. He tells me, "We can use Harrold's place."

Diane, the waitress with the Woodstock baby, comes from an old gaming family. Her father, Harrold, is the head of the MGM slot department. Tommy says Harrold keeps a one-bedroom apartment in a building across the street from the hotel just for such liaisons.

Harrold not only uses the apartment himself, but loans it out to his friends, who pay for the privilege with boxes of cigars and bottles of cognac and champagne. Harrold is always on the make, and I know a couple of waitresses who have been to the apartment. One tells me, "The closets are empty except for shelves of porn films."

I've met Diane's mother, an Ava Gardner-looking woman who was a dancer at the original El Rancho Vegas. I like her and wonder if she knows what her husband is up to.

Today my flip retort is, "It's against my religion—Lutheran girls can't do it when the moon is full."

\* \* \*

Alice experiences her own kind of stress. At each pit where she and Diane are doing breaks, Alice sneaks a drink.

Ronni and Diane watch her become someone not in the real world. They watch Alice pick up an order at the Casino Bar, walk through the pit, oblivious, take more orders, pick up glasses, walk to the Cub Bar, drop off all the drinks she just picked up, get the new order and repeat the process. She makes all this activity look efficient, but it's like watching Jiminy Cricket on speed. Ronni says, "In forty minutes, she never delivered one drink."

In addition to drinking, Alice has become heavy into uppers and downers and is snorting a lot of coke. To escape from her life, I guess.

Ronni and Diane begin to cover for her.

One day Alice, Ronni, and Diane are scheduled to do pit breaks. This shift begins at noon. At five minutes to twelve, Ronni and Diane come out of the dressing room to head for the escalator that leads to the casino. They see Alice coming toward the dressing room. Alice, in another world of her own making, can't speak a coherent sentence.

"Oh God," Diane says, "do you think we ought to try to get her dressed?"

Ronni shakes her head and says, "How are we gonna get her dressed?"

They follow Alice back into the dressing room. They help her to sit down. Diane says, "Call Lenny."

"Oh God," Ronni moans. "I don't want to call Lenny and tell him she's screwed up again."

"What else can we do? We can't leave her here alone like this."

Ronni heads for the wall phone.

From her seated position, Alice's head falls forward and she slumps to the floor.

Diane screams, "Son of a *bitch*, she's stopped *breathing*!" She gets down on the floor and begins to give Alice mouth-to-mouth resuscitation.

Ronni's voice is high-pitched as she tells the hotel operator, "We have a cocktail waitress in the dressing room who's passed out. We need paramedics. *Now!*"

Ronni is panicked, but Diane says, "Go in there and get some paper towels and real cold water. Keep slapping them on her face and under her arms and on her wrists."

The wall phone rings. Ronni answers. On the other end of the line, Milton yells, "If you girls are not on the floor in five minutes, *you're fired!*"

Ronni takes a deep breath and says, "Milton, do you realize we've got Alice in here, and she's quit breathing? We're waiting for paramedics!"

Milton slams down the phone.

The paramedics storm into the dressing room. Diane moves back and they slap an oxygen mask on Alice's face. They remove her blouse to bare her arm. When they try to give her the IV, blood squirts everywhere, all down the front of Diane, all down the front of her red uniform.

The phone rings again. This time Milton screams, "I want you girls on the floor! You've got no business—the people are there, they're taking care of it. You get up on the floor!"

Ronni stammers, "Diane—Diane's covered with blood—you know—it squirted!"

Milton must think red on red sounds okay, but blood has a tendency to turn dark when it dries. Leaving Diane to sponge the blood off her shoulders and bodice and skirt with wet paper towels, Ronni hurries up the escalator to the casino. Thirty minutes later Diane appears on the floor. Her uniform doesn't look good, but she's there. Milton slaps her with a warning notice for being late.

The paramedics take Alice to the hospital, she recovers, and the next day returns to work. While the rest of us watch helplessly and do our best to cover for her, she continues her erratic, drug-induced behavior.

## CHAPTER 18 – Blackmail


On Arline's days off, Lara does pit breaks with Alice. Alice exhibits strange behavior that makes Lara wonder what's messing her up. Alice tells Lara she's recovering from a terrible automobile accident, and, "That's why I'm sometimes so goofy."

Lara complains, "She gets an order, goes back to the bar, and has no idea where she is, or where the order goes." Lara tells her to just stand at the bar, and she will cover for her.

Alice asks, "You know anybody who's got any dust?"

A drug called Angel Dust is hitting the streets, but nobody we know has tried it. Lara defers the question, but Alice presses. "I don't know," Lara says. "I guess I could find someone who has some. I'll ask around."

Lara goes to the Dice Pit waitress Fran, who's known to be dealing marijuana and coke. Fran has a child being raised by her parents and needs to give them money. Lara says, "Fran would probably have plenty of money if she didn't spend so much on romance novels." Lara buys the dust from Fran and sells it to Alice for the same price.

"It's not really dealing if you don't make any profit," Lara says. "And I just want her to get off my back."

A few days later Lenny calls Lara into the bar office, blows smoke in her face, and slams the door shut.

He gets into her face and says, "I could kill you, but I won't do it myself, I'll have it done."

Lara can see by the color of his face that he's serious.

"This girl better never—*ever*—come into this place fucked up again or it's your ass! You're a dead bitch!"

Lara whispers, "What are you talking about?"

Lenny says, "Alice told me you're the one that's giving her the drugs."

"Lenny, y-you're out of your mind," Lara says, stammering. "I-I thought she was in an accident. I thought she was having strokes or something. I didn't know she was on anything."

"She says you bought it for her."

"One time," Lara admits. "Just once, a favor because she kept asking me. One time, that was it. I *swear*."

Lenny snarls, "If she ever walks in here fucked up again, you're dead."

Lara realizes the door is shut—there's nobody else to hear what he says. For days she's afraid to start her car. She doesn't say anything to Alice, figuring Alice will just deny she said what Lenny claims she said.

Lara prays Alice will get her act together, and soon.

* * *

The MGM hires a consultant to enhance the hotel's image. The woman decides that the cocktail waitresses should wear a rhinestone beauty mark on the left cheek.

She shows us how to affix them with eyelash adhesive. Because your cheek skin moves every time you speak or smile, the damn things keep falling off. They begin to appear on the floor, on the service bar counter, in ashtrays, on your tray, in drinks.

Players ask, "What's that thing on your face?"

Another question for which we feel compelled to invent a smart answer.

I'm on a break in the ladies' bathroom fiddling with a tube of eyelash glue when Dor comes in for her break. She plunks her tray down next to mine and says, "Guess what? Haley got her job back."

Haley, the cocktail waitress in the Parisian Bar, is a young mother with two children and a predilection for expensive perfume, real jewelry, and unemployed musicians. She lives well and has the reputation for being able to stretch a dollar till it screams in agony.

When there's talk about Haley, Arline says, "She's got the first buck she ever stole."

Haley has been fired for stealing. Both hotels and union take stealing quite seriously and are diligent in fact-finding and back-up paperwork to support any such claim.

"The union got her job back?" I ask. "How did that work?"

"The union had nothing to do with it." Dor's grin reminds me of a pretty Cheshire cat, all teeth and sly-lidded eyes. "Haley saw Alice and Lenny together in the San Jose airport."

I put the cap back on my tube of eyelash glue. "Well. They must be having an affair, then."

"Yup. That girl blackmailed Lenny to get her job back in the Parisian Bar."

I stare at Dor through the mirror. "God, that's an incredible rumor. Are you sure? Why, that could get all over the hotel."

Even bigger Cheshire smile. "I certainly hope it does."

I laugh. This is the best rumor in several days. "I'll do my part."

This particular day I am doing pit breaks, which takes me to both ends of the casino. In the next hour, I tell this story to five other girls, some of whom had already heard that Haley has gotten her job back. Between the blackmail angle and the affair, this is a hot story, guaranteed to entertain everyone for days.

In Pit Two, the floorman gets a phone call. He gestures to me and hands me the phone. It's Lenny, and he is not happy. He wants to see me in his office, "*Now.*"

When he sees me coming towards him, he chomps tighter on his cigar and says nothing. He turns his back to me, and I follow him into his office. He slams the door. His face is the color of overcooked beets.

"*What the hell* are you telling everybody about Haley and Alice?" he screams. "*What the hell* right do you have to say things you don't know anything about? Who the *hell* do you think you are? *What the hell* do you think you're doing?"

I don't know why I feel so calm. I guess it's that I honestly don't feel I've done anything wrong. I simply repeated a rumor, and I tell him so.

"Oh, Lenny, you know how those casino rumors are." I figure making this into a joke is a good bet. "They come and go from moment to moment. You shouldn't take it seriously."

That makes him even angrier. I can tell because he takes his cigar out of his mouth—something he never does—and shakes it at me. He leans forward, and because he's much shorter than I, he now has to look up to yell in my face.

"Do you realize I could *sue you* for libel?" He pauses to get his wind.

I pray that while I'm alone with him in this office he doesn't have a stroke.

He shouts, "You get the *hell* back up there on that floor, and you tell *Dorothy to get her ass down here!*"

I go to Baccarat, where Dor is working. I tell her Lenny wants to see her in his office right away. I tell her how upset he is about the Haley/Alice/San Jose rumor. She must be a little shaken, because she says, "God, what'll I say?"

"You just go tell him the truth, like you told me to always do. You told me you heard it from Haley in the Parisian, and you just go down there and tell Lenny that's exactly where you heard it. That that's what happened. What can he do? He can't sue anybody for libel if it's true."

"You think?"

Now I'm not so sure. I hesitate, then say, "No, I don't think he can."

A half hour later, Dor comes back. I'm relieved to see she's laughing. "Boy, is he pissed!" she says. "He told me I'll never work in the pit again."

Lenny pulls this same screaming and threatening act with Haley, who swears she never told Dor anything. I can understand that she wants to cover her ass, because with two kids, Haley needs the job. But how else could Dor have found out? Considering the only sources are Haley, Lenny and Alice. Lenny is out. Can't ask Alice because it's her day off, but it's unlikely she will say anything. So Dor has to be telling the truth.

It occurs to me that during all of Lenny's hollering and threatening, he never said the story wasn't true.

\* \* \*

Jayda, a tall black girl, works in slots. She's single with no children, but living with her is a little sister with some kind of physical disability. She has several sisters and brothers who also work in various jobs in the casino industry. Her parents live nearby.

Jayda makes no attempt to hide the fact that her whole family is into voodoo.

Fran tells Dor this, adding, "Now some things are really going to start. By the way, do you know Kathleen Woodiwiss' has a new book?"

Dor has no idea what she's talking about.

The next morning Dor opens her locker and finds a voodoo doll hanging from a bent coat hanger. It's a rag doll made with the same red velour as our costumes. It has no facial features, but tufts of scarlet hair are glued to its head. Sticking out of the body are several pins, each one a different color.

Dor won't touch it.

I know gamblers are superstitious, but voodoo seems archaic, like something from another time that is out of place here. Maybe that's what makes the doll so horrifying. "God, are you sure that's your hair?" I ask.

"Positive."

"How do you think they got it?"

Dor wears her red hair in ringlets that fall to her shoulders. "Somebody must have cut a piece when I was standing still talking to somebody and not paying attention." She seems to have it all figured out. "I can't believe this."

Dor locks her locker, goes to the food and beverage office and tells Milton about the voodoo doll. I don't know what she expects, but she feels she needs to tell somebody who might be able to do something, though she doesn't know what.

Milton says, "Pulleez. We're tired of your shit."

Jane shuffles some papers on her desk, avoiding Dor's eyes.

Lenny stares at Dor in disgust. "Get out of this office and go to work."

Dor returns to the dressing room. She unlocks her locker. The doll is gone.

"A copy of my key could only have come from the bar office," Dor reasons. "Now, they're trying to scare me out of here."

I don't understand why we can't all just come to work and do our jobs and go home, and I tell Dor so. Now I'm on my own rant: "What is it about this business that breeds such personality conflict, such jealousy, such malice? Is it really all about money and sex? Who has it and who doesn't? Who's getting it and who isn't?"

This makes Dor laugh. "Yes," she says.

Now Alice confides to Diane that the reason she has such a problem with pills and liquor is that she loves Lenny so much, and he is still with his wife, and so she doesn't know what to do with her own life. On and On.

While diapering coffee glasses in the Reef service bar, Diane tells us this story. "She thinks Lenny's the love of her life."

Arline snickers. "Hardly the dick of your dreams."

I feel sorry for Alice, but these are her choices. It just makes me sad to watch on a daily basis as a woman hurts herself. And for what?

* * *

Lara throws a plant party to introduce a friend of hers, Richie Geller, who has just opened Plant World, Las Vegas' first live houseplant shop.

Del never goes with me to any parties attended by cocktail waitresses. He says he's "not a party person." He likes plants, but I can't even drag him to see them.

Richie has brought in big plants in heavy clay pots to decorate Lara's house. The plants are lush, with shiny green leaves, because they've just been trucked in from Los Angeles and have not yet reacted to the dry desert air. Lara's living room is crowded with people, drinking and talking loudly. All this greenery draws attention away from Lara's second-hand furniture.

Lenny and his perpetual cigar sit next to her on the couch. He's not here for plants. He teases and touches until Lara becomes fed up with his advances.

Sitting nearby, at the edge of the fireplace, Diane and Alice act like nothing's going on.

Lenny rises to go to the kitchen to refill his glass of Mateus, weaving his way around several dieffenbachias.

Lara pours herself another glass of wine from a bottle on the coffee table and says, "Jeez, that Lenny is such an ass. My God, he's greasy, he's dirty, he dresses bad, he blows cigar smoke in your face." She takes a deep drink of the wine, half emptying her glass.

She's so pissed at Lenny that she doesn't notice that Diane and Alice are not reacting. She rises from the couch to turn up the sound on the record player, and John Lennon's *Whatever Gets You Through the Night*" intensifies.

"I don't know how anybody could fuck something like that," Lara continues, waving her wine glass for emphasis. "You couldn't pay me enough."

The next day Diane takes her aside and says, "Those things you said last night about Lenny, in front of Alice—"

Lara, now sober, says, "What?"

"You didn't know Alice and Lenny are sleeping together?"

"You're kidding!" Lara breaks into a fit of giggles. "Oh. My. God."

* * *

Before a weekday shift, Arline, Ronni, Diane and I meet for an early breakfast at Alexander's, a pretty restaurant in the new Alexander Dawson building on Flamingo, east of Maryland Parkway. This building business complex, with fountains and outdoor cement benches, is one of the first to be completed on this recently-widened section of Flamingo Road.

It's rumored that the builder, Alexander Dawson, has also constructed a complete underground house on the lot across the street, where only grassy mounds, a few short trees, and some new bushes are visible.

Our topic of the morning is the latest casino gossip, the revelation that Lenny and Alice are having an affair.

Diane, who has been working pit breaks with Alice, is relieved. "I always knew Alice had a secret lover," she says. "I never asked because I thought it was my father."

## CHAPTER 19 – All About control

In each pit a floorman peacock-struts, his eyes hired to watch the games. The floorman keeps track of the play and accordingly doles out comps for free food and shows and rooms. If a player wants female companionship, the floorman doesn't arrange for that. Female companionship is generally arranged through a hotel bellman, and it is not free.

A pit clerk—always female—processes the credit "markers" that players bring from the casino cage. The floorman also watches the dealers, to make sure no one is stealing.

The pit boss for that particular gaming pit watches the floormen.

The shift boss, in charge of all games on the shift, watches the pit bosses.

The casino manager, Morrie Jaeger, watches the shift boss.

Everyone is watched by hidden security cameras in the pastel frescoed ceiling, commonly referred to as, "the eye in the sky."

Because it's the 1970s and the media is full of equal-rights issues, the MGM Grand wants to be seen as an equal-opportunity employer. Jaeger's assistant, Vic Wakeman, is a dwarf. Wakeman is just as nattily dressed as every other casino boss, only in exquisitely-tailored miniature. Behind his back he is commonly referred to as, "the eye in the rug."

Traditionally, drinks served to players in casinos have always been presented by sexy, young things. In keeping with 70s thinking, the MGM and the union decide men should not be barred from jobs serving cocktails. This leads to the hiring of the first-ever cocktail *waiters*.

When Arline hears we're getting a guy to serve cocktails, she muses out loud about his costume. "Do you think his skirt will be longer? Do you think they'll cover his chest?"

Tall, soft-spoken, 37-year-old Jimmy Henderson joins our day shift as cocktail waiter in the Keno Lounge.

Prior to becoming a cocktail waiter, Jimmy was a Keno runner at the MGM. He became the first male Keno runner in Las Vegas because of his long-time friendship with Keno Manager Tony DiIorio.

One day Danny Litwack spotted him and asked him if he'd like to be a cocktail waiter. Jimmy tells us, "I said, oh yeah. Think of the tips I'd make."

The bar office hired Jimmy and then three other men. Jimmy rolls his eyes to the painted cupids in the ceiling and says, "Lenny told us he wanted male cocktail waiters because girls have periods and call in sick."

The four of them are sent to work the cavernous Jai Alai fronton. They run up and down the cement grandstand stairs, sweating in the heavy red jackets. "We made no money," Jimmy says. "Most people bought their drinks before they came to their seats. I couldn't wait to bid on something else and get out of there."

He's spared a male version of our bellboy dresses. He wears black slacks, a white tux shirt, a black bowtie and a red brocade jacket with a black satin rhinestone-studded collar. He does not have to wear the jaunty pillbox hat.

After the first week, the sleeves of his jacket get so dirty the bar office instructs the wardrobe mistress to cut them off, so that now instead of a jacket, Jimmy wears a red-brocade vest.

Jimmy has never served cocktails before. He doesn't know drinks or brand names or the appropriate garnishes. When a woman ordered a Virgin Mary, he told that bartender she wanted, "a Bloody Virgin." I remember my intense week of Bunny training and the Playboy Club's drink ordering system and pity the harried bartenders, even Tommy.

"Frank Sinatra taught me how to open champagne," Jimmy tells us. "I was really young, working room service at the Frontier. He took it out of my hands and said, 'Here, I can see you're really struggling with that. You don't know how to open the damn thing.' He gave me a black chip and a signed satin jacket."

Jimmy entered our casino cocktail world when he bid and won a shift in the Parisian Bar. His first mishap was to spill a screwdriver on Muriel Rothkopf's pastel pantsuit. On his second day, he waited on his first hooker. "They come into town when they're on their periods, you know, from the Chicken Ranch." He laughs when he tells us she ordered something called a "chaz walsh", but he knew Chaz Walsh was the MGM swing shift casino manager. "She told me what the drink was, but I was confused," he says.

Jimmy quickly becomes the darling of all the cocktail waitresses. He takes everything seriously and then surprises us with outrageous comments. His gay wit fits right in with our variety of bitchy, gossipy personalities.

Female gamblers love Jimmy, too. He gets his share of sexual harassment. Women often pinch him, and a few even cup his crotch.

One day Lenny assigns him cash-bar breaks. In the Coffee Shop, a man with a face of pock-marked skin asks Jimmy, "Are you one of those queer fags? Is that why you're a cocktail waiter?"

Jimmy says, "Do you know how you can tell if somebody's gay?"

He has the guy's interest. "No. How?"

"They have faces with a lot of pits."

* * *

The day shift boss in charge of the blackjack pits is Dixson, the man of the tailored suits, tastefully tinted glasses, impeccable sideburns and surly attitude. When Dixson is in the pit, the girls stay as far away from him as possible. They spend a lot of time at the service bar, or somewhere else outside the pit, waiting for the "clap" call.

When a player wants a drink or a floorman wants coffee, and there's no waitress already in the pit, the floorman raises his arms and with his hands makes a loud clap. The waitress enters the pit, and he tells her what table to take drink orders from. Usually while you're there you can take orders from surrounding tables as well, so that you can come back from the bar with a full tray. Full tray equals more tips.

If he's a nice floorman like Jerry or Wally, you don't have to wait for the clap—you can enter the pit any time and hustle all the tables for drink orders as much as you want. Of course, the more drinks you serve, the more chance you'll get tipped, and the more money you make.

Stern, unfriendly Dixson is known for his bad attitude toward cocktail waitresses.

Arline says, "I think he was going out with a girl on swing, and she must have used him or something. After they broke up, he hates everybody."

"Wait till he's working a pit where Jimmy shows up," Ronni says. "That'll be fun to watch."

Dixson isn't the only man in my life who thinks cocktail waitresses are scum—I get the same subtle messages from my own husband. Del drops comments like, "Don't believe everything those airheads tell you," and "She needs a man to tell her what to do", and "You know, half of them are hooking."

I stop telling him about things that happen at work. I don't even want to imagine what he'll say if he learns about Jimmy.

One day I come home from the library with some currently popular feminist books: French philosopher Simone de Beauvoir's *Second Sex* and journalist Letty Cottin Pogrebin's *How To Make It in a Man's World*. I drop them on the coffee table and head into the kitchen to start dinner.

I'm peeling potatoes when Del comes home. When I hear him come in the front door I wipe my hands and go to meet him. In the living room I see him looking at my library books.

"I'd be careful what I read if I were you," he says.

"What?"

"You know how easy you are," he says. "You believe everything you read."

Here we go again. I know this is all about money and control. An unspoken issue between us is who controls the money. Most cocktail waitresses bring home more money than their husbands.

When Mia gets engaged, she happily proclaims that her Greek fiancé told her that after they're married he will not let her work. A week later she says that he's decided to let her work, after all.

"What changed his mind?" Diane asks.

"He discovered how much money I make."

## CHAPTER 20 – Dor's dilemma

Clap your hands and a beautiful girl comes running. What a subtle way for a man to feel powerful and in control.

Dor enters Pit Two with a tray load of drinks, sees Dixson striding from another direction toward the same entry point—a large space between two tables. She doesn't want to call attention to herself, so she sidesteps to make way for him. She misjudges both distance and balance. Her tray—hot coffee, drinks, Bloody Marys, ashtrays, money, chips, napkins—tilts and spills across the roulette table. To avoid the disaster the roulette dealer jumps sideways. The spin must be voided.

A big man with a big voice, Dixson swears. Several people look up from their cards and laugh. Blackjack dealers turn their heads slightly to catch the excitement, but they know better than to laugh. Luckily, there's no broken glass in the roulette wheel.

Dor picks up her tray and scrambles to recover her tips. She picks up some napkins and tries to mop up the mess.

Dixson screams, "Get *out* of the *way!*" He grabs her upper arm and shoves her out of the pit.

At the end of the shift when Dor, whose skin has begun to bruise where Dixson grabbed her, goes to sign out, Jane is alone in the bar office. She's been left to hand Dor her latest warning slip.

"Jane couldn't look me in the eye," Dor tells me later. "I think she's embarrassed to have to be giving me these things. Those guys are such pussies. Now they don't even hand them to me themselves—they make her do it."

Dor figures this warning slip has to do with the accident at the roulette wheel, but no, it's for something much worse.

It's for stealing. She's fired.

Two days later, Mariella, who worked cash bar breaks the day before, tells Lenny it's not true that Dor is stealing. "How can you steal when you're giving away free drinks?" she insists. "Dor wasn't even working any of the cash bars on the date of the infraction written on that warning notice."

Lenny doesn't want to be confused by facts. The problem is, petite Mariella has a tall drinking issue. Lenny tells her he knows about her sneaking drinks and if she associates with—even is seen *talking* to—Dor, she will be fired. Never mind the logic that since Dor is no longer working on the floor it's unlikely Mariella will be seen talking to her.

Mariella calls Dor at home to tell her how she tried to defend her, and that Lenny wouldn't hear it.

"I'm sorry," Mariella tells Dor. "I can't do any more. I have two kids. I can't afford to lose my job."

Dor goes to the union and makes a formal complaint to Al Bramlet. Papers are filed, phone calls are made, and Dor gets her job back. But Lenny, furious, doesn't give her back her newly-won pit station—he puts her in the coffee shop.

"Now you know what makes him mad?" Dor grins. "I make money in the coffee shop. I work my ass off with cocktails. Other girls just stand there, but I hustle everybody. I talk to everybody. Jaegar sends people into the coffee shop with drink comps, and they give me big tips."

Dor knows how to work her scarlet curls, giant smile and outgoing personality to the hilt. Customers love her. Still, the coffee shop is not the pit.

Dor is headstrong and relentless. Back to Bramlet. She demands to be fully restored, which is her right by contract, to the shift assignment she had when Lenny came up with the stealing story.

Dor tells me all this over lunch in the Help's Hall.

"But you know Bramlet," she says. "He works a lot under the table."

"What does that mean?" I ask, piling my plate with fancy finger sandwiches left over from a banquet the previous evening and now available to employees.

"He's on the take, from the hotel. Hey, those things look good." She selects a few of the little sandwiches for herself. "You know, to let things pass. He's always trying to get me to let things pass."

"How?"

We carry our plates to a nearby table and sit. With one fingernail Dor removes the sliced black olive atop the egg salad spread on one of the sandwiches. "He says, 'Do you think maybe we should get you a good job in another hotel?' I told him, I have a good job. And he said it doesn't seem like they're going to let up on me."

Dor doesn't understand why Bramlet can't force them to let up on her. "Everybody knows he's one of the most powerful men in town," she says.

"And isn't that part of what union membership is for?" I ask. "To protect you when the management wants to fire you just because they don't like you?"

She says that more than once Bramlet has told her, "We'll get out there next week." When "next week" comes, something always comes up, and he can't make it.

"It's an old-boy thing," Dor says. "A girl really has to fight for her rights."

Months pass before Lenny gets an official call from the union telling him to put Dor back in her pit station. Like lots of male egos, his is not happy with being told what to do. Stubborn about complying with the union mandate, he gives her pit breaks. When the pit breaks are completed, he lets other pit break girls go home early, but not Dor; he makes her go back into the coffee shop to finish out the shift.

* * *

Lenny is having a bad day.

During the night, an anonymous caller phoned his house. His wife answered the phone, and the female caller informed her that her husband is sleeping with Alice. Now he likely has unwanted decisions to make. Things are not going well at home.

In Lenny's mind, Dor is his nemesis. He is convinced that she is the one who has ratted him out to his wife. He did not personally hear the woman's voice, but no matter—his mind is made up.

"That makes no sense," I say to Dor. "There's nothing in this for you. Why can't he see the big picture? Sure, he doesn't like you, but who has the most to gain when the wife finds out he's cheating? Who's madly in love with him? If Lenny answers the phone, she hangs up. If the wife answers, she says her piece and hangs up. The wife doesn't know her voice."

Alice.

* * *

On her day off, Dor goes to the Aladdin to visit her juice friend who knows Lenny, casino manager Jimmy Don. Happy to see her, Jimmy Don takes her into the coffee shop to buy her lunch. They slide into a booth near the entrance, reserved for management because it has a long cord with a handy telephone.

"I just want to tell you what's happening at the MGM," Dor says to him.

Jimmy Don snaps his fingers at a nearby waitress, and she delivers two menus. "I've heard." He laughs. "Lenny told me you're a real bitch, a real troublemaker."

Over his corned beef sandwich and her crab salad, Dor tells him the whole story, about all her warning slips, about Lenny and Milton following her all over the floor, about Lenny firing her for stealing, about the phone call Lenny thinks she made to his wife.

Jimmy Don says, "Lenny told me that you told a lot of people he wanted to go to bed with you."

"Because it's true."

"He says not."

"Why would I make up something like that? About him? He's trying to justify what he's doing to me." Dor picks at her salad. This whole situation embarrasses her.

They eat in silence for a few minutes. Finally Dor speaks. "I just want to say one thing."

Jimmy Don looks up from his sandwich to listen.

"This is just between you and me. I want you to know I never did any of those things Lenny told you I did. And I appreciate you getting me the job, and I'm sorry I made it such a hell, and I wish I'd never taken it."

Her friend calls the waitress to bring the lunch check for him to sign. "Well," he says, "I believe only half of what he told me, because you worked in my hotel for a couple of years and never caused a problem."

Dor can see that this is as far as the subject will go. Her juice won't fix this. Bottom line—Jimmy Don and Lenny are friends.

"It's the way it is," she tells me later. "Men are men and women are women."

* * *

When Dor's uniform goes missing from her locker, she gets another warning notice. If she doesn't pay the hotel for it, Lenny threatens to call the police and have her formally charged with stealing hotel property.

Not only is the bustier dress missing, but also all the pieces that make up the uniform: collar, cuffs, panties, belt, hat. According to Lenny, a $100 value. Dor agrees to let payroll deduct the money from her paycheck. Two weeks later, they add it back onto her paycheck. Lenny tells her it is because she has to pay in cash.

Back to the union. Dor tells Al Bramlet about this latest problem.

"Just pay it," he advises. "Don't worry about it, I'll get it back for you."

Dor goes to the bar office, where Jane presents her with a paper itemizing the missing uniform pieces. She hands Jane a one-hundred-dollar bill and leaves. There is no receipt.

Weeks pass.

Dor has a date with a man who happens to be a lawyer, and over their lobster dinner she mentions how she had to pay for this stolen uniform.

Her date says, "Legally, they can't make you pay for the uniform. That's why they put it back on your check. Then you paid them cash. No one ever got that money except whoever you paid it to."

Bramlet never gets back for her the c-note.

## CHAPTER 21 – Party animals

Early on the day of July 3, 1975 for several hours a summer rainstorm deluges Las Vegas. The Charleston underpass closes, a deep depression in the street now flooded with six feet of water. Someone in construction didn't manage well an ancient desert flood wash, and more than 300 cars float off the Caesars Palace parking lot, causing over $1 million in property damage. Two people are killed. To handle claims, representatives from major insurance companies set up tables in the Caesars Palace lobby.

But it's my day off and this afternoon the sun is out. I have hennaed my hair, and in direct sunlight I resemble a big red, Irish Setter. Red hair may look striking on Dor, but it's not my most flattering color. I'm more of a washed-out Irish Setter. Still, I feel glamorous, and I like how the different hair color makes the colors of my wardrobe look more vibrant.

This afternoon, bartender Kevin, four other cocktail waitresses and I bar-hop down the Strip, surveying the rain damage. By 2 p.m., we're all trashed, except for Karen.

Karen, whose deceased father was a clean-up man for the mob, is a mid-twenties brunette who has been in A.A since she began working seven years ago—underage—as a cocktail waitress at Caesars Palace. She's not one of those born-again alcoholics who loudly protest if you drink around them—a good thing since she makes her living serving cocktails. Karen just stays quietly sober.

We're all piled in my Caddy, which Del has had painted Wedgewood Blue. I'm at the wheel, careening down the Strip. This catches the attention of Metro's finest. "Metro" is what the police are now called, since the Clark County Sheriff's Department and the City of Las Vegas Police Department merged in 1973 to become the Las Vegas Metropolitan Police Department.

Lights flash. I pull over.

Quick-thinking Karen whips gum out of her purse and passes a piece to each of us.

In the back seat, Kevin slurs, "Lemme talk to 'em. I'll straighten 'em out."

Karen hisses, "Keep Kevin quiet back there."

No matter how messed up you are, I think some kind of adrenalin thing kicks in when you're confronted by a cop. Your bodily reflexes might be slow, but I believe your mind sobers up several notches. I show my driver's license and car registration. Along with the adrenalin I feel a sudden cold realization: if I get a ticket, there will be no way Del won't find out. He will tell Paul and Jeff and Neil and Bill and I will never hear the end of it.

Today the God who protects little children, stupid people, and drunken cocktail waitresses is looking out for me. I'm not asked to step out of the car. I don't get a ticket—just a verbal warning—and Kevin keeps his mouth shut.

* * *

I read somewhere that Halloween has now become, after Christmas, the second biggest commercial holiday.

We schedule a Halloween Party for October 27 at the clubhouse at Louis Prima's golf course, Fairway to the Stars. Because of its location, out of town in the desert at Warm Springs and Bermuda, Fairway to the Stars isn't so popular with golfers. But we couldn't find a location in town that we wouldn't have to pay for, and it's a great place to have a party. At night, no one will appreciate this oasis of green in the middle of nowhere. But the clubhouse sports lovely white Grecian columns and lots of overstuffed couches.

In the high desert of Las Vegas, the fall season happens for two weeks: the second and third weeks of October. By Halloween, Las Vegas experiences full-blown winter weather.

There's a lounge show on the Strip with a clever skit where three girls come out dressed as short old men who dance. Their costume consists of a big top hat that rests on their shoulders and covers their faces. Waist to knees is a shirt and jacket, and little baggie pants extend from the knees down to floppy, fat-toed clown shoes. They dance with their arms behind their backs, because their naked torsos are painted faces. Their bare boobs are painted eyes, and when they move it looks like eyes are sweeping around the room. Cute and clever.

For the Halloween party, the girls press me to dress as one of these characters. I consider it, but the weather is cold. I'm not willing to expose my tits to the winter elements. Instead I don jeans and a painted jean jacket, and tell everybody I'm an "undercover narc."

At the party, we present pre-arranged skits—and drink. News and entertainment figures prominently in costume choices.

Diane comes as Tammy Spraynet, a take-off on the reigning first lady of country music.

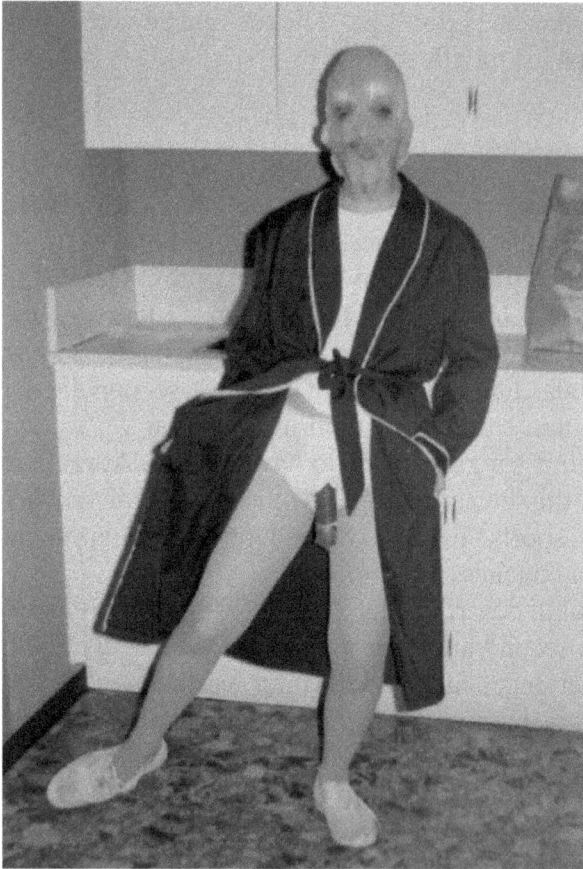

Ronni is a flasher in a plaid flannel bathrobe, complete with a real salami in her white men's jockeys.

Arline comes dressed completely in camouflage and fake gun, and tells us she's Patty Hearst. Berkeley college student and granddaughter of newspaper magnate William Randolph Hearst, Patty Hearst has been in the news for being kidnapped by a neo-revolutionary group, the Symbionese Liberation Army (SLA).

Dor does a skit dressed as the housewife, Laverne, Cher's famous character from *"The Sonny & Cher Comedy Hour."*

Bartender Kevin cross-dresses for *The Kansas City Bomber's* K.C. Carr, a role made famous by Raquel Welch.

Lily and Betty come as bubbles.

In a song-skit Jimmy parodies—complete with high-tear dramatics—Tammy Wynette's hit, *"Stand by Your Man",* loses his balance and topples onto a guy in the audience who is in a wheelchair.

At the end of the evening, Ronni the Flasher is so drunk she drives her car onto the darkened golf course and can't find her way out. Deep wheel gouges in the turf assure that next year our group will not be able to come back for a Halloween party at Fairway to the Stars.

Me as an undercover narc & Arline as Patty Hearst

\* \* \*

My fellow dayshift cocktail waitresses schedule a gathering for breakfast at a newly-opened restaurant on East Sahara, The Library. Old English lettering on the outside sign makes it look like a pub. Inside the décor mimics a traditional English library, complete with dark paneling, overstuffed chairs, and shelves of leathery-looking books that nobody reads. Just inside the front door a huge stone fireplace dominates the cocktail lounge.

The menu even has steak and kidney pie, but without the kidneys.

"I love steak and kidney pie," I say to our waiter. "But how can you call it steak and kidney pie if there're no kidneys in it?"

Straight-faced the waiter, in his clipped accent, says, "Americans won't eat kidneys."

No breakfast with this group of girls would be complete without your choice of early morning alcohol, such as a Bloody Mary or a shot of Amaretto in your coffee. By 10 a.m., an hour before we are all due at work, everyone except A.A. Karen is cheerily tipsy.

This is when Lily announces that we should call Lenny and "give him the what-for."

Helluva idea.

She'll even make the phone call. Ronni volunteers the dime.

When Lenny answers the phone, Lily tells him the entire day shift is too drunk to come to work today. "Besides," she says, "we deserve an extra day off."

I'm sure Lenny can hear us in the background, giggling and howling with booze-induced laughter.

Lenny screams, "You all better be here *on the dot* at eleven or *all your asses'll be fired!"*

Yes, we have had a lot to drink. But that does not stop us from racing in cars down the strip to make it to the MGM on time. No one is fired. Amazingly, no one is even written up for coming to work drunk. Not even Dor.

\* \* \*

Diane announces she is going to have a baby. Her family is thrilled, including her six-year-old Woodstock son. For months on our days off, Ronni and I work to sew a cotton quilt of appliquéd baby alphabet letters.

Del has sold the Wilderness in its permanent spot at the Lone Palm and improved our status as American homeowners by buying a modular home at 3914 Katie Avenue, a block from Chaparral High School. It's farther to drive to work, but we have an acre that can be subdivided. By selling the other half acre Del gets back all of our down payment.

Our modular home on Katie Avenue, with my Caddy in the pea gravel driveway

Now I fill my spare time with decorating our new three-bedroom, two-bath home. Del and I both like antiques, and enjoy shopping together for old furniture. I fill every room with plants. The hip décor of the time is Victorian, and I add lots of lace curtains.

Thickets of tamarack trees surround the house. They drop a lot of needles that create a fire hazard, especially in the hot summer months. When I catch three Chaparral students in the trees smoking grass, I confront them. They're stunned when I take the cigarette from them, take a hit, and announce, "You should know a cop lives here. Hiding in the trees is suspicious." I take another deep drag from the joint. "If you want to smoke this stuff, do it walking down the street, where no one will pay any attention to you." I never see them again.

Reading is not one of Del's pastimes. Besides critiquing my choice of reading material, he criticizes the music of the seventies. He hates Eric Clapton's current hit, *"I Shot The Sheriff."* The sixteen-year difference in our ages feels like it's widening, but I'm still attracted to his dark humor and the can-do, take-charge, devil-may-care-ness about him.

Del refuses to hang his bailiff's uniform in the closet. Instead, he hangs it on the outer door. "If anyone robs us," he says, "I want them to know upfront they're robbing a cop."

He tells me that if he's not home and some guy breaks into the house, I should shoot him dead. "If he falls outside the threshold," he adds, "you drag him over it into the house. And be sure he's dead, so it's only your story. Otherwise he'll say you picked him up at the hotel and invited him over. Cocktail waitresses do that all the time."

The inside of the modular is very seventies: all dark wood paneling and olive green carpeting. I now have over sixty houseplants. It's the perfect setting for my first house party.

I offer our new home for Diane's baby shower on November 5. Not at all interested in seeing his home overrun with cocktail waitresses, Del disappears for the evening.

Diane and her mother love the quilt that Ronni and I have made. This is the first time I have had a chance to chat with Diane's mother. She is a gracious lady, still quite beautiful, and when I look at her I wonder if she knows about her husband's secret apartment.

\* \* \*

Del invites one of the attorneys he has met at the courthouse, Bob Miller, over for dinner. A six-foot-plus, husky, soft-spoken guy, Bob is the son of prominent Las Vegans Ross and Coretta Miller. Bob's wife, Sandy, would have been invited, too, but she has gone to Europe with friends for two weeks.

This is the first time Bob and Sandy have been apart since they were married and Bob is not a happy husband. I have the impression he had let her know that he did not want her to go, but she went anyway.

I cook Del's favorite Polish dish, Chicken Paprikash, and we have a pleasant evening—Bob is interesting to talk to.

After he leaves, Del predicts, "Trouble in paradise" for the Millers. I like Bob Miller and I am happy when later Del is proven wrong.

\* \* \*

As Thanksgiving approaches, bar chatter centers around who has the day off, who is dining where and who is cooking what.

Mia announces that for her Greek fiancé she plans to cook a Greek turkey.

I didn't know they had turkeys in Greece. "How do you stuff a Greek turkey?" I ask.

Arline steps up to the bar just as I voice this question and announces, "From the rear."

Mia grabs her tray and stalks off in a tiff, insulted on behalf of all women who sleep with Greek men.

* * *

Del and I spend Christmas Eve with Jeff Silver at Paul and Charlene Goldman's, along with their daughters Gillian, Julie and Heather, and a standard-sized, matted, black poodle.

Christmas Day I work my regular day shift at the MGM. A running joke with the floormen and bartenders is that what they want for Christmas is "pussy." So I have baked sugar cookies with a walnut half on one side surrounded by chocolate sprinkles. All day, to much hilarity, I hand out my "pussy cookies."

For New Year's Eve, Del and I go to Ronni and Harry's for a party in their ranch home way out of town off Tropicana on Carruth, two blocks past Eastern Avenue.

Ronni and I have taken a bread-baking class, so we meet at her house on New Year's Eve morning to assemble the party food. We laughed and gossiped our way through the bread class without paying a lot of attention, and the bread we bake for New Year's Eve comes out like beige bricks.

Ronni sighs and says, "We'll never be able to compete with Mormon housewives."

Forget the bread—we will take a break in her living room with mimosas. The house, in a new subdivision of Lewis homes, is one

Paul on the piano with Jeff on harmonica.

**Del and I at Christmas**

of the first to have a vaulted ceiling. I sit down on the couch and look up to where the opposite wall meets at the ceiling peak.

"Is that daylight I see through there?" I ask.

Ronni laughs. "Harry's real pissed about that. But that's what you get with Lewis construction."

\* \* \*

Besides our love of arts and crafts, Ronni and I have in common older husbands. Del and Harry are about the same age. Del and Harry talk "ain't it awful" about the fuel crisis and terrible economy—though I am making more money than ever before in my life. To please our husbands and save money by not dining out, Ronni and I start a domestic routine where we alternate Tuesday evening dinner and game of pinochle at each other's homes.

Del and Harry accuse Ronni and me of cheating at pinochle. After several weeks of denial, Ronni and I figure, why fight it? We work out an elaborate system of subtle gestures for each of the card suits. We don't win that many more games, but our husbands seem to enjoy it more when they catch us cheating.

Ronni has a good friend she worked with on the front desk at the Aladdin, Tansy. Tansy has become engaged to Four Queens Entertainment Director Ron Bell. Ronni opens her home for Tansy's wedding shower. Ronni and Harry own a sixteen-millimeter movie projector, and Ronni decides it would be great fun to show a porno movie at the shower. She finds an adult store on Paradise Road, next to the Cinema Arts where *Deep Throat,* starring Linda Lovelace, is in its tenth week.

The evening of the wedding shower, forty-six women crowd into Ronni and Harry's two-story tract home. Del has come along to keep Harry company in the kitchen. After the champagne, ice cream, cookies and cake are served and the living room is littered with bows and ribbon and wedding wrap, it's show time.

The first reel of Ronni's porn choice is loaded onto the projector. The lights are lowered. Lots of nervous giggling accompanies the grainy, black-and-white opening scenes.

In the hallway, Harry says to Del, "Is this legal? Are we going to get arrested?"

* * *

Ronni and I are working in Pit Two. Pit Three is scheduled to open an hour later, at noon, with Lily and Rhonda scheduled to work there. We look forward to working together with them off the Reef service bar.

At 12:30, Pit Three is open and there is no sign of the cocktail waitresses. Five minutes later, here comes Milton. Because he's short, when he walks fast he looks like he's bouncing. He wants to know "where the hell" Lily and Rhonda are. As if Ronni and I would know.

We get the scoop later from Jane.

At 12:45 p.m. Lenny gets a call in the bar office. It's Rhonda. She and Lily have been up all night, drinking. They don't just quit—they take turns on the phone telling Lenny what an asshole he is, how all the girls despise him, how stupid he is, how they have better things to do with their lives than waste time working at the MGM Grand, etc. etc.

At 1:10 p.m. they call Dixson. Every day they worked with this man, as soon as he arrived he would order them to bring him a scotch on the rocks. They hated it every time this man grabbed their asses. They hated it every time this man said something lewd under his breath as they passed by. They hate this man with a vengeance.

When they get Dixson on the telephone at the pit clerk's desk, they tell him they want him to know that they've quit. "We want you to know that every day we've been spitting in your scotch." Dixson is shocked, livid, and helpless in the knowledge that he will never know if Lily and Rhonda are telling the truth.

Today Ronni has to bring him his scotch. When she hands it to him, he looks at it, but doesn't take a sip.

"Is there something wrong?" Ronni asks.

Dixson has the pinched look of a man who's had one too many face lifts. He says, "You been spitting in this, too?"

## CHAPTER 22 – Star players

Some players you never forget—especially the stars.

Lucille Ball is in the hotel filming a CBS TV special called, "Lucy Gets Lucky." In the 60-minute segment, she plays Lucy Collins, an obsessed Dean Martin fan, determined to see him even though his appearance at the MGM Grand Hotel in Las Vegas is sold out. When Lucy Collins learns that Dean Martin plans to do a show just for the employees—we real employees know this would never happen in a million years—she gets a job as an MGM cocktail waitress.

Lucille Ball is 62 years old. The average MGM cocktail waitress is 25. The TV costumers must think that all you have to do to erase three decades is to put a woman in a full body stocking.

Hotel customers are just as stupid. Flame-tressed Dor serves a round of drinks in the 21 pit where they're shooting. When she comes out, she gets stopped on her way to the bar.

"Gee, I love your shows."

"You always make me laugh."

"Can I have your autograph?"

Dor can't hide her amazement. "What's *with* you people?" She stops short of reminding them how old Lucille Ball is.

Somebody on the crew sees this and tells Miss Ball. At the end of the day's shooting, she introduces herself to Dor and says, "Isn't that awful, they think you're me." She smiles at Dor. "A young thing like you."

Dor is impressed with how gracious Lucille Ball is.

"I wish I did look like you," the star adds, "then I wouldn't have to cover all this skin with this horrible body stocking."

* * *

Body builder/actor, Lou Ferrigno, television's *The Hulk*, comes into the hotel wearing a tee shirt, shorts and flip-flops. You can tell he is the Hulk because you can see green paint that didn't wash off around his toenails.

"Gee, he's so short," says Karen. "Somehow I thought he'd be taller."

* * *

On nights when there's a roast in the Celebrity Showroom, many movie stars use the Parisian Bar as a kind of Green Room, the place to wait for their turn to go onstage. Jimmy entertains us with his stories of good stars/bad stars. Dean Martin is "George", he says, casino jargon that means he tips well. Jimmy has learned the lingo along with the drinks.

"Jerry Lewis is the worst, always complaining about everything." I've heard this about Jerry Lewis. He doesn't seem to have a good reputation around town. "And what a cheapskate," Jimmy adds.

He adores Elizabeth Taylor. "She ordered a scotch and soda with a twist, then sent it back saying it was a terrible brand of scotch. The bartender put an extra ice cube in it and sent it back, and she was happy. Very gracious. And absolutely beautiful—not that tall, but such big feet."

* * *

Everyone's heard that Burt Reynolds has very little hair. Is it a toupee, or is it real? When Dor serves him a drink in the Cub bar, she makes it a point to walk all the way around his chair, peering closely at his head.

She presents a check for him to sign—Burt Reynolds has a comp and doesn't have to pay. She leans over to pick it up and feels a tug on her skirt.

"What are you doing?" she asks.

Burt Reynolds displays his boyish, hard-to-resist grin. "I wanted to see if you had any underwear on. It looks like there's nothing there."

Dor is glad that this day she has remembered to wear the Danskin panties.

"But his hair really is a toupee."

\* \* \*

Naturalist outdoorsman Euell Gibbons appears in Pit Two. A television celebrity and spokesperson for Post Grape Nuts cereal, he's known for authoring three best-selling '60s books: *Stalking the Wild Asparagus, Stalking the Healthful Herbs*, and *Stalking the Blue-eyed Scallop*.

He's not all that lucky at blackjack, and maybe not all that healthy—he dies soon after his visit to the MGM, at the age of sixty-four.

Euell Gibbons does not tip dollars or casino chips; he tips little brown acorns with his name printed on them.

Bad player.

\* \* \*

Independent Nevada gubernatorial candidate James Ray Houston shows up in Pit One. He owns a company called Western Pacific Gold & Silver Exchange. He's also the author of a cheery little book called *Countdown to Depression*.

"I read it," Arline reports. "I wasn't all that impressed."

He tips me a green chip ($25).

Good player.

\* \* \*

Cincinnati Reds' baseball player Johnny Bench is playing blackjack in Pit One. Johnny Bench has lots of awards like National League Rookie of the Year, Most Valuable Player (twice) and the Lou Gehrig Award. He's also known for a spectacular home run in a 1972 final game vs. Pittsburgh.

Of course, all the casino floormen and bosses know who Johnny Bench is. The hotel often broadcasts sports events like baseball on television monitors hanging from the ceiling around the bars. Woebegone for the cocktail waitress who, while taking a drink order, blocks a floorman's view of a TV monitor—a serious casino sports offense. Jayda is the only waitress who never gives a thought about anything like this. She lapses into a lazy grin and says, "I's de token Black."

Johnny Bench, small-town baseball guy from Binger, Oklahoma sports a boyish grin guaranteed to make any girl want to take him home and play mother.

Lily asks him for his autograph, "for my brother." Johnny Bench asks her out to dinner. They go to Benihana at the Hilton. Lily says, "It wasn't much of a date. Everybody stopped him for autographs."

* * *

Lara notices the guy sitting at the Cub Bar, watching her coming and going as she serves drinks in Pit One. He asks her out. She giggles and blows him off. She has no idea who he is until her brother-in-law, a swing boss in Baccarat, tells her, "He's a nice person. Go. Don't you know who he is?"

Lara shakes her head. "No."

"That's Johnny Bench."

Lara giggles. "So, who's Johnny Bench? Who cares?"

She goes out with him, more than once.

One day we are all working together off the Reef Bar service station. "Are you fucking him?" Ronni asks her.

Lara giggles.

"I'd fuck him in a New York minute," Ronni presses, hoping to win Lara's confidence.

For days we all speculate on whether or not Lara is having sex with Johnny Bench. Lara giggles a lot, but she's not talking. We conclude that she is having fantastic, hot sex with Johnny Bench.

* * *

In Pit One, Isabella waits on a rich Texan, decked out in a white suit and cowboy hat. He's betting with five-hundred-dollar chips, and has been at the same table for two hours.

In an attempt to break the Texan's winning streak, the floorman changes out the dealer. The departing dealer swipes one palm over the other and raises his hands, palms outward in the air, the standard gesture to show he has no chips or money in his hands. As he leaves the table, the dealer whispers to Isabella, "You and I could really work this guy."

"What do I need you for?" Isabella asks.

The Texan is in the middle of a big play when Isabella, carrying a tray of Bloody Marys, trips and spills them down his back. The pit boss whisks away the white cowboy suit jacket to be cleaned by the hotel. He banishes Isabella from the pit for the rest of the day. She feels terrible about the white coat and no more tips from the Texan. However, Isabella is happy that she doesn't get a warning notice.

* * *

One Saturday I'm pulled out of the pit to do cash-bar breaks. This is an annoying inconvenience because I did not come to work with a bank with which to make change. I do the best I can with what tips I have already made in the short time I was in the pit.

In the Parisian Bar I wait on a couple. He orders a Tom Collins and she orders an orange juice. I notice the dress she's wearing because it's my favorite color, magenta. With her auburn hair piled in fat curls on top of her head, the woman is attractive, but she has the look of a displaced mid-west secretary.

A few hours later, I arrive to break the waitress in the Cub Bar. A couple comes in and sits down. I approach to take their drink order.

"An orange juice," the woman says. I recognize the auburn curls and the magenta dress.

The couple from the Parisian Bar. Here's my chance to be Superwaitress.

To the man I say, "Don't tell me—you're having a Tom Collins!"

The man looks at me, eyebrows meeting in the center, perplexed. "God, no," he says. "Bring me a scotch and water."

Oh my God. I realize this is not the same man the woman was with in the Parisian Bar. She scowls at me.

I realize I've just waited on my first hooker.

* * *

Waiting on celebrities doesn't mean anything. Sure, it's interesting to see what they look like up close and personal—like the chance to inspect Burt Reynold's rug. I'm usually surprised to discover a lot of celebrities are shorter than I am. But many stars are cheap—meaning they don't tip. Often they exude an attitude that they're doing you a great honor just to be near them.

It's a nice surprise when a celebrity turns out to be a pleasant person. Lara waits on a lot of stars. She seems to have star-attraction. Singer Glen Campbell, quiet and polite, tips her a red ($5). Comedian Lonnie Shore she calls, "The sweetest sweetheart in the world."

Comedian Myron Cohen is one of her favorites. He sneaks up behind her and whispers, "Would I love to tickle your fancy." Lara giggles. He adds, "I've got somethin' that'd tickle you to death."

Everyone loves comedian Jonathan Winters, who seems to have a built-in smile. And what's not to like about teen heart-throb singer Pat Boone?

* * *

The beautiful Australian singer Helen Reddy is appearing in the Celebrity showroom. She is only two years older than I, and some people tell me I resemble her. I am sure it's just the dark hair and the haircut, but it is flattering to hear.

Her husband, Jeff Wald, regularly plays blackjack in Pit One. To look at him—just an average-looking guy, not very tall, with an unmemorable face—you would never suspect that he is the high-powered Hollywood talent agent with the reputation for being a coked-up wild man.

Jeff Wald tips well. A flirtation begins with Isabella, our favorite flashy-eyed Cuban cocktail waitress with the long, red nails. Isabella sleeps with Helen Reddy's husband and he buys her a gold necklace. Someone ought to write Helen Reddy a new song, "*I Am Woman—With Philandering Husband.*"

Lara says, "What can he possibly see in Isabella?

"Her healthy teeth and come-hither smile?" I ask.
Lara smirks. "She has no tits."

\* \* \*

Las Vegas itself becomes a star player when the newspapers announce, "Tourists & Press Inaugurate the Las Vegas Celebrity Train." Departures will begin in September, 1974 for Los Angeles' Union Depot. The inaugural run will feature Milton Berle as guest conductor and will cost $74.95 per person/double occupancy, plus tax (of course). It will depart on Sundays at 3 p.m. because hotel check-out time is noon.

Then—nothing. No more is heard about the short-lived Las Vegas Celebrity Train.

## CHAPTER 23 – Anniversary week

Because the MGM Grand opened in December, the first week of that month is designated to celebrate the "Birthday." Months in advance, the bar office announces that during Birthday Week there will no extra days off, no allocated vacations, and "nobody better call in sick." December of 1975 marks the hotel's second anniversary.

I want to take a vacation the first week in December and go home to Seattle to visit my parents. As soon as I learn about the anniversary week restrictions, I begin to make an alternative plan.

On Sunday, the beginning of anniversary week, my father calls to tell me my mother has gone into the hospital. She is weak and not responding to her medication. The family doctor is concerned.

A year ago, my mother had open-heart surgery. She has never been strong, and at sixty-seven, she doesn't have the motivation to do the prescribed physical therapy and has not recovered as fully as expected.

By itself, the fact that she has gone to the hospital is not unusual or alarming to me. A teen-age victim of rheumatic fever, my mother has been in and out of hospitals all her life, nearly dying from abdominal surgery when I was three years old and the doctors left a sponge inside her body. Many a day I have spent hanging around hospitals with my father—resulting in my belief that hospital cafeteria food is good.

"I'll ask for next week off," I tell my dad. I figure he'll probably be able to use some help when she comes home from the hospital. I call the airlines to get last minute round/trip/Seattle fare quotes.

The next day, I'm sitting in the ladies' room on my break. Here comes Betty, who flounces down next to me and announces that she is off tomorrow on a vacation with her husband, Mike. "Wait a minute," I say. "This is anniversary week. You can't take time off."

Betty doesn't miss a beat. She also doesn't look at me. "Oh, Lenny's already approved it. Mike made the arrangements." This is the husband who works upstairs in accounting. This is the only time he can go, Betty explains.

Oh, the unfairness of it. A lot of people don't like following rules. I'm not one of them. I don't mind rules. I just expect them to apply equally to everyone. If no one can take time off during anniversary week, I expect the "no one" to include Betty, no matter who she's married to and in what department he works. I don't know about how this no-time-off-during-anniversary-week rule applies to the accounting department, and I don't care.

I don't say anything. Best not to rock the casino/cocktails boat. What do I really care if she goes off this week, anyway?

On Tuesday I get an emergency telephone call at the hotel from my father. "Honey, your mother has experienced respiritory failure."

My mother is dead.

Tears stream down my face. I walk into the bar office in my uniform and tell Lenny, "My father just called to tell me my mother died. I'm leaving now to fly to Seattle to be with him. I don't know when I'll be back."

I don't give a shit about anniversary week. I don't give a shit about rules. I don't give a shit about the MGM. I don't give a shit about Lenny. I don't give a shit if he fires me.

To my surprise, he says, "You go, Carolyn. Don't worry about a thing. Do what you have to do." To my greater surprise, he removes the cigar from his mouth and adds, "I wish I could see my parents one more time."

## CHAPTER 24 – Sex in Sin City

After work Dor, Lara, Ronni, Arline and I are having drinks and an Italian dinner at the Bootlegger on Eastern and Tropicana. Ilsa, a German girl who works in slots, is the hot topic of the moment. She has met and married a Southern millionaire.

"Why her?" Lara ponders. "She has no tits."

Dor says, "Between his accent and her accent, how can they understand each other?"

A big myth about being a cocktail waitress in the most expensive hotel in Las Vegas is that you will meet a millionaire who will "marry you and take you away from all this." One girl in 133 accomplishes this, and everyone believes there is hope for all.

Except I don't believe it. The waiter brings more red wine, and I say, "What refined, educated millionaire is going to marry a cocktail waitress? Only in Las Vegas is cocktails considered a desirable professional career. In the rest of the country, people think cocktail waitresses just sling drinks because we can't do anything else."

Lara raises her wineglass in a toast. "Well, I can't do anything else."

"Who would want to do anything else?" Ronni asks. "Look at the money we make."

Lara says, "Ilsa wasn't making money in slots. She was making something else."

"If you want to meet and marry an old millionaire," I say, "get better odds. Get a job in a men's clothing store in Palm Springs."

Arline adds, "Or move to Alaska."

Lara, who is modestly endowed, raises her wineglass again, and says, "I always thought you had to have tits."

\* \* \*

Ronni attracts the attention of a man of prominence in the community, a member of the large Lamb family. He's tall, an accomplished horseman, and has appeared in movies that were filmed in southern Nevada, such as *The Gauntlet* and *The Ballad of Cable Hogue.*

Ronni is attracted back. Major flirting ensues.

They want to have an affair, but they have a dilemma. They can't agree on a time to liaise. He wants to meet in the daytime, when his wife thinks he's at work. Ronni works days and wants to meet in the evening, when Harry is at work in the Aladdin showroom. On Mr. Lamb's days off, he's with his wife and family. On Ronni's days off, she's with her husband and daughters. After weeks of outrageous flirting and frustration, they are deadlocked. There is no affair.

\* \* \*

One Saturday night, Ronni and I attend a going-away party at the Social Circle lounge, across from the MGM, for a dealer who has quit.

The next two days, Sunday and Monday, are my days off. Monday night Ronni calls me. In her voice, I can hear plotting. "Listen, I got this con going," she says, "and you've gotta keep it up for me." Ronni's days off are Tuesday and Wednesday.

"What'd you do?" I ask, knowing whatever it is, it will be entertaining.

"Well, I told Tommy that Saturday night after the party you and I took a dealer home and had a three-way."

In general, when a casino conversation is not about sex, it's about money; when it's not about money it's about some form of sexual act, idea or illusion.

"Which dealer?"

She laughs. "That's just it. I told him we were so drunk we can't remember who it was." She describes how she would stand at the bar, look out across the pits and, in front of Tommy, say things like, "Could that be him? Oh, I'm so embarrassed. No, maybe it was that one over there…" Then she would add little allusions to what sexual things we did with him.

She goes on to tell me she got Tommy so horny by dragging the story out all day that by the end of the shift he was smashed on vodka.

I go to work on my "Monday" and arrive at the Reef service bar where I am confronted by a churlish, spiteful Tommy. It's only 11 a.m. and he is not a happy bartender.

His approach today is surly and argumentative. He harasses me with questions: "So you and Ronni had a good time Saturday night? Which dealer did you do? How many times did you do him? Did you really do all those things Ronni said?"

I give him my most teasing smile. "Gosh, Tommy, that was two nights ago. I'm not sure he told us his name. I don't think I'd recognize him this morning."

"Sure, you'll get drunk and do him, but you won't do me." He reaches for the vodka bottle.

I keep this sexual charade going all day Tuesday and all day Wednesday. When Ronni comes back on Thursday, Tommy is so incensed by the idea that we fucked some dealer we can't remember, but won't fuck him, that he's no longer speaking to either of us.

* * *

Ronni lives every day—and night—to the max. One night we're out with the girls bar-hopping, I turn around, and there she is, giving head to a dealer seated on a bar stool. She has a regular player boyfriend who comes in six times a year on a junket from Chicago. He brings her little gifts, like diamond earrings. She tells Harry that she got them on sale at Joseph Magnin. One summer night she takes her player to Sunset Park. It's after midnight, and they are going at it, naked on a blanket, when the automatic sprinklers come on.

Another time she takes him to dinner at Jeremiah's Steak House on Tropicana. "Give us a dark corner in the back," she tells the hostess.

There are only two tables in the back and the hostess leads them to the one that is unoccupied.

"Jeesh," Ronni says. "My eyes get accustomed to the dark, and there at the next table is my brother, his wife, and their two kids."

\* \* \*

These extracurricular activities slow down when Ronni takes Stewart, a dealer in Pit Two, as a regular lover.

Ronni and Harry are building a house on horse property in the desert south of town, and between construction, horse management, raising two daughters, a full-time job and now a new local lover, this is one busy woman.

The bar office changes Ronni's days off. Now they are the same as mine. The very first week that we have the same days off, we plan to drive to Los Angeles for a shopping expedition. At our Tuesday night dinner/pinochle game, Del says to Harry, "I suppose now that they have the same days off, we won't see much of them."

I want to visit my favorite La Cienega fabric shop, Home Silk, and Ronni wants to order custom-made English riding boots. We've scored some uppers called "mini-whites" so we can waste as little time as possible sleeping.

Ronni knows a fast shortcut out of town. Instead of taking the I-5, we drive all the way out two-lane Eastern Avenue, turn right at Lake Mead Boulevard and pick up the freeway there. For the five-hour drive down to Los Angeles, we exchange stories, babbling non-stop. Same for the five-hour drive back.

Ronni can't say, "no" when Stewart wants to meet her in LA. He flies down, arriving shortly after us, and we meet at the motel.

We shop, we lunch, we shop some more, we have dinner, we go to see Jane Fonda's new movie, *Barbarella.*

Stewart can't keep up with us. During the movie he falls asleep. Next day we're up early to do it all again, nonstop, driving all over Los Angeles. By the end of the day, he's irritable and touchy—he hasn't gotten laid. He swears he'll never "go shopping" with us again.

Ronni often visits Stewart in the West Tropicana trailer park where he lives. Stewart doesn't cook, so when she finds a tray of homemade lasagna in his refrigerator, she is quite surprised. The next day she arrives at the trailer early—he has given her a house key—and while she's waiting for him, the phone rings.

She answers. A woman asks for Stewart. Ronni says, "You know, he can't come to the phone right now. He's really, really sick."

"Oh my god," the woman says. "What happened?"

"I think it's food poisoning," Ronni says. "He ate some bad lasagna."

\* \* \*

Everyone knows about Diane's father's infamous apartment across the street. The girls decide that we should go in together and rent a place of our own, a generic place where a girl can take a guy when she just wants to fuck him, not let him into her house or her life.

It's a slow morning at the Reef Bar. Between drink orders, the conversation goes like this:

Ronni: "What part of town? It should be central."

Dor: "We sure don't want to be across the street in the same building as Harrold."

Arline: "You guys need to really think this through."

Ronni: "We have. Say $200 a month for a really nice one-bedroom, divided by ten girls. That's just $20 a month per person. I'd put in that."

Arline: "You have a steady boyfriend. You'd use it more than anybody else."

Lara: "I like Regency Towers."

Arline: "Too expensive."

I say, "Should be near some good restaurants. A girl's gotta eat."

Arline: "What if a girl quits? Does she still get to participate in the apartment?"

Ronni: "If she pays her $20. Why not?"

Dor: "How about Mount Charleston?"

Part of the Toiyabe National Forest, Mount Charleston is a 7,000-square-foot-plus mountain recreation area thirty-five miles northwest of Las Vegas. It's where you go in winter to ski Kyle Canyon and drink hot chocolate laced with Grand Marnier while you sit around the big stone fireplace in the alpine ambiance of the historic Mount Charleston Lodge.

It's where you go in summer to escape endless days of 100-plus temperatures. Waterfalls, campsites, picnic areas, fifty-two miles of hiking trails and all that fresh mountain air attract everybody. Tucked away in the pine forest are numerous cabins and homes. On the mountain, there is no grocery store, no gas station. All provisions have to be driven up from Las Vegas.

Lara giggles. "Oh, a cabin at Mount Charleston would be sooooo romantic."

Arline: "You want to be romantic or you want to fuck?"

Lara: "Can't we do both?"

Ronni: "My brother knows a dealer who has a friend who has a place up there. It has a fireplace."

Lara: "Ooooooh, a fireplace!"

Arline: "Too expensive."

Ronni: "I'll ask him if he knows of anything available to rent."

Me: "Are you guys crazy? Mount Charleston? That'll be romantic around the fireplace in the winter, all right, with snow outside. But what about driving back down the mountain, like in the middle of the night?"

Lara: "What do you mean?"

Me: "That highway 157 is fucking dangerous. It's a two-lane road that winds all over the place. Slick in the winter. Accidents happen. Hell, accidents happen on that road all year round."

Lara's eyes widen. "Accidents?"

Me: "How're you going to explain to your husband that you got in an accident with another guy in a car coming down from the mountain at two in the morning?"

Lara: "Never thought of that."

Me: "Better stick closer to home."

Arline: "Probably why Harrold has his apartment right across the street."

In the end, it is all sexy talk and no action. For four days it has provided something fun to talk about. But no one wants to be responsible for under-the-table babysitting, that is, find an apartment, negotiate a lease, sign a lease, manage the use time, and collect every month from the other girls.

\* \* \*

At dawn Lara opens up her house to a group of MGM day-shift horseback riders. She lives on an acre on Pecos Avenue, where there are no street lights and the nearest neighbor is not within calling distance.

This area is zoned Ranch Estates and everyone who lives out here except Lara owns a horse. Lara's house is ten years old, a simple, white, three-bedroom, single-story house with a fireplace where she lives with her seven-year-old daughter.

A floorman, a couple of dealers and some of the cocktail waitresses—including long-nailed Isabella—regularly head out into the desert to ride at dawn among the Joshua trees, sagebrush and yucca.

I do not know much about horseback-riding, but I wonder how Isabella can saddle, mount and dismount a horse and handle reins with those nails.

Lara brews coffee in a big restaurant-grade urn, and in the fall builds a fire in her fireplace. After the brisk, early morning romp through the desert, the riders tie their horses at a hitching post in front of the house, and come in to enjoy coffee and donuts around the fire. It's all fun and impressive. Then everyone is off to work.

Isabella is a regular, but other waitresses roam in and out of the group.

Lara, who is not a horsewoman, confides, "Those casino cowboys get a lot of pussy."

These are not men of interest to Lara and Ronni.

\* \* \*

One morning Ronni comes to work and tells me how she and Lara seduced Donald. A floorman in the Dice Pit, Donald wears black, horn-rimmed, Clark Kent-like glasses, so they call him, "Superman." Donald obeys all the rules and rarely lets the girls into the pit to hustle drinks.

Lara calls him, "So proper—a real pain in the neck" and vows to "get him."

This week, Donald's wife is out of town, and Lara invites him over to her house for a drink after work. Donald accepts.

"We raped him," Ronni recalls with a laugh. "But it got out of hand. He turned into a wild man! He made a lot of noise, and he has this thing about *biting* your pussy."

To Ronni and Lara it is worth being sore for a day or two because now they can "take the Dice Pit" any time they want, any time they're scheduled to work there. Their tip income takes a dramatic increase.

For years Superman and his wife have been trying to get pregnant. Now suddenly, she's pregnant. Months pass and she gives birth to a healthy baby. Ronni and Lara buy baby presents and personally deliver them to Superman's house.

"You've got some balls," I say.

"We got quite friendly with his wife," Ronni tells me. "Poor Donald was a nervous wreck the whole time we were there."

"I wonder how that woman can walk after he gives her head," Lara says. "He's such a chewer, such a biter."

Their next target is Weird Wally. They convince me that I should join them for a ménage à quatre. We will have it at Lara's house on the evening her seven-year-old daughter has been invited to a slumber party. Wally can't believe his luck when we begin to tease and pester him, promising all sorts of sensual delights if he can come to Lara's that evening.

I don't know what he told his wife, but he couldn't say "yes" fast enough.

* * *

For Mariella's birthday Lara throws a party at her home. Half the plants Lara bought from Plant World have died, but she still has an impressive collection. The Mateus is flowing and the air is thick with cigarette and marijuana smoke. Her stereo is loud with the sounds of Patti LaBelle, KC & The Sunshine Band, the Doobie Brothers and the Bee Gees. Luckily this far from town she has no close neighbors to complain about noise levels.

Lenny and Alice have not been invited.

Cozied up next to me on the couch is my bartender nemesis, Tommy. The conversation around us lulls for a moment and he says, "So, Carolyn, when are we gonna fuck?"

Several of the girls turn to stare at him.

I have had enough of this, and a fair amount of Mateus. I stand up in front of everybody, look down at him and say, "How about right now?"

The look on his face says he's startled. He recovers, stands and says, "Okay, let's go."

"Fine," I say, challenging him. "Let's go."

Leaving our friends speechless, I head for the front door. Tommy follows. We climb into his red Porsche. He heads for Boulder Highway, where there are a lot of rent-by-the-hour-with-porn-television motels.

Next day Ronni says with a smile of satisfaction, "I can't believe you did that, right in front of everybody. I loved it! He ought to treat us all better now."

## CHAPTER 25 – Culinary strike, Latin for "vacation"

I listen to the talk from the waitresses working with me off the Reef service bar and realize three of them are dating powerful guys involved in culinary union activities. Karen is dating union president, Ben Schmoutey, Kim is "close friends" with Al Bramlet, and Mariella is dating Gramby Hanley.

Though Ben Schmoutey is president, Al Bramlet—of the brushy mustache and scraggly comb-over—is the real power behind Culinary Union Local 226. Nevada is a right-to-work state, but over the years Bramlet has negotiated wage increases and benefits until the state is ninety-eight percent union-organized. Bramlet has made it possible for lowly culinary workers like maids and porters and cooks and dishwashers to buy homes, to enter the middle class.

Bramlet owns businesses that get contracts from Strip resorts—common practice among Southern Nevada public officials and not illegal if reported to the National Labor Relations board—making him a millionaire. He's a likeable guy, and a lot of people like him because they owe him. It is understood that he is so powerful that not even the Chicago mob, trying to claim a bigger share of Vegas, can touch him—though one of mob enforcer Tony Spilotro's thugs has threatened his life.

Gramby Hanley and his father, Tom Hanley, are reputed contract arsonists. Culinary union pickets are a regular sight in front of the non-union Alpine Village Restaurant on Paradise, and on the roof on a Saturday night in December, 1975 two bombs explode. On a sunny Monday morning in January, 1976, when a bomb blows up David's Place, the new non-union gourmet restaurant on West Charleston Boulevard, it is said all over town that the Hanleys did it. Booby-trap bombs are also set in cars outside of the Starboard Tack restaurant and our favorite hang-out, the Village Pub, two restaurants also involved in labor disputes with the union.

With such blatant activities and relevant talk, you would think that police detectives would be all over it. There is some newspaper coverage and a show of a big investigation, but no arrests are made.

"I went to school with Gramby Hanley," Ronni tells me. "He used to stick a gun in kids' car windows and demand their money."

When she sees him at the Reef Bar talking with Mariella, she freezes. Gramby, in a hip, long-sleeved black shirt with white polka dots, sits on a stool nursing a bourbon and water, in no hurry, and watches Mariella with hungry-wolf eyes. Brazen Mariella flirts with him.

Ronni avoids him until he leaves, then approaches Mariella.

"Do you know who that is?" she whispers.

"Of course," Mariella says, "That's Gramby Hanley. He's my boyfriend."

Ronni pales. "Do you know how dangerous he is? What you are getting into?"

Mariella smiles the smile of a woman in fresh infatuation. "Oh, he's changed," she says. "He's not like that anymore. He writes poetry."

Ronni stares at her. She can't believe Mariella's naïveté.

"He's really a sweet guy." Mariella stares off into the spacious casino. "He bought me a mink coat."

* * *

The union and the Las Vegas hotels cannot agree on a new contract.

Al Bramlet waves a hand, and on Thursday, March 11, 1976, Culinary Union Local 226 goes on strike.

This is my day off, and Del and I are leaving for dinner at the Bootlegger when Ronni telephones to give me the news.

"They came in at a quarter to seven and told us we were on strike and had to leave. A massive walkout. Jimmy had a tray of drinks to serve and Bramlet told him to just set his tray down and forget it." She's laughing, like it's all some kind of joke. "I had a full tray, too. Bramlet just said, 'Put the drinks down. You're on strike.' So we left."

She says when they went downstairs to change their clothes they were told that Bramlet wanted them to go right out on the Strip and walk with picket signs. Some of the girls, who had dates later, had worn to work their mink coats. "There they were," Ronni says, "on the Strip in their mink coats and high heels, carrying *signs*, for God's sake."

"What do we do now?" I ask.

"Nothing, I guess. Wait to hear."

The hotels are paralyzed. They remember that four-day disaster back in 1970. They had not believed that anybody would strike, so they refused to bargain and locked out the unions at thirteen hotels. Culinary Local 226 and Bartenders Local 165 walked out of the International, the Desert Inn and Caesars Palace.

Now Musicians Local 369 and Stagehands Local 720 have joined the culinary and bartenders' unions. Fifteen resorts are affected. Newspaper editorials speculate that the Culinary union runs Nevada state government.

Arline, still dating her younger dealer, tells us that he says, "Management is all scared Bramlet will somehow also organize and unionize the dealers."

No one has any idea how long we'll be out of work. Our union rep says we have to picket on the street in front of the MGM. Twenty hours a week to get "strike pay"—a pittance—from the union.

The day we are scheduled to begin picketing, Ronni, Lara and I drive to the hotel in one car. We park at the side of the hotel and walk to the Strip. A long, erratic line of people—of all colors— meander down the sidewalk, carrying strike signs. We don't see any other cocktail waitresses, only the maids and porters and cooks and dishwashers.

Then we spot Kim perusing the crowd. She sees us, waves and walks over.

"We are *not* walking the streets with these people, like some kind of hookers," she announces. "I'll fix it."

We can't find our union rep to sign in, so we go home.

Kim goes straight to Al Bramlet.

Next we hear from our union rep that cocktail waitresses can picket on the side street, at the MGM employees' entrance; we do not have to walk the Strip with the unwashed workers of "Mole City."

The union rep is there with a clipboard. We are expected to sign in, picket for four hours, and sign out.

Nobody asks about strike pay. After all, how much can it be? As cocktail waitresses, we get paid an hourly wage, but our major income is from tips. Whatever salary we get means little. We view it as pocket change. The bi-monthly paychecks are so insignificant that most of the girls often forget to pick them up.

Ronni once got a call at home on her day off from a cranky woman in the payroll department. "You have five paychecks here," the woman informed her in an icy tone. "You have to come to the time office and pick them up. They expire after ninety days. It'll be a mess of paperwork if we have to reissue them."

Arline never picks up her checks. When the woman from payroll calls, she tells her she has the wrong number and hangs up. Since her first job out of high school Arline has never filed a tax return. She says, "If you never file, they'll never miss you."

The girls quickly work out a "vacation exchange" schedule: I'll sign in and out for you for X number of days, then you'll do the same for me. We will all cover each other. The union rep doesn't know or recognize every girl by name and sometimes he sends a "representative" with the sign-in clip board.

This makes sense to everybody. As Lily reasons, "Why show up every day if you don't have to?"

* * *

Too lazy to carry picket signs, Ronni, Arline, Karen, and I gather in my kitchen and paint big black "ON STRIKE" letters on white sweatshirts.

My father comes down from Seattle for a visit. On March 19, someone covers my sign-in responsibility while we take a day trip to Hoover Dam.

Since cocktail waitresses are "excused" from picketing on Sundays, we plan a Day Shift Family Picnic in Paradise Park for Sunday, March 21. It will be the only time that everyone can gather with their kids together during the day to party. The picnic is a well-attended, fun success, with softball and hot dogs and lots of beer.

Our strike news comes from reading the newspaper and talking to our union rep. Bramlet is now so busy he doesn't have time to talk to cocktail waitresses. We don't take this strike all that seriously, anyway. We are on "vacation."

The air at the MGM employees' entrance, where a sturdy chain link fence separates cocktail waitresses from the rest of the world, is festive. We sit in the shade in the back of Fran's van and read, gossip, knit and do needlepoint. A coffee wagon, arranged by someone who knows someone, makes a regular morning round just for us.

Fran is reading Kathleen Woodiwiss' *Shanna* and has another girl reading *The Flame and the Flower*. Arline thinks they are frivolous and refuses to discuss literature with either girl.

Mariella brings thermoses of coffee laced with Amaretto.

Fran brings marijuana brownies.

I am hand-sewing a spool bedspread that will later win a purple Grand Champion ribbon in the Jaycee State Fair.

Alice is knitting an afghan for Lenny.

As the spring weather improves, some girls arrive in bikinis, spread out blankets on the pavement, and work on their suntans.

On Thursday, March 25 my father and I take off for a few days to visit Scotty's Castle in Death Valley, California.

* * *

Our union rep says we can apply for food stamps. With no idea how long the strike will last, some of the girls decide to do it. Together they drive out to an office in Henderson to do the paperwork. They report back that this is a humiliating experience.

"They treated us like shit," Karen says. "They said, 'Oh you don't have any money? We know how much you girls make,' and they wouldn't qualify us."

Ronni discovers, however, that for some reason—three kids?—she "qualifies."

"I have a husband who is a Maitre d', for God's sake," she says. "He's working."

I do not understand this business of being on strike. The politics of it are murky. In the newspaper, both hotel execs and union men regularly contradict themselves. I read their quotes and think they sound just like regular politicians—lot of words saying nothing. None of it makes any sense at all to me.

Even my father, a lifetime member of the Teamsters' Union, does not understand the issues, whatever they are.

* * *

Our union rep informs us that there is going to be a vote on a new contract. On Saturday, March 27, the entire union membership will go to the convention center to register their vote. This will be accomplished in three shifts, so that the convention center is not overly crowded at any one time.

I think we're going to vote on a question that asks, should we continue to strike or shouldn't we? And to write yes, that we have read the proposed new contract. But the way the actual paragraph and question are worded is convoluted. It reminds me of the newspaper quotes. None of us understands the verbiage of the motion. "And we are cocktail waitresses, for God's sake," says Ronni, "Who knows how the maids and porters will interpret the words?"

Most everyone voting on the first shift votes to accept the contract. Then rumors begin to fly about the "truth" of what we've been told. Outside the convention center, Mexicans and Blacks picket against the contract. By the third shift, most everyone votes against accepting the contract.

I have been raised to believe in the power and good of workers' unions. Going through this strike disillusions me.

"The way it's been handled looks like one big fiasco," I say to my father.

He shakes his head. "I can't explain it," he admits.

I become depressed to realize that I have no idea what the vote means. I have no idea how they count the votes to determine an outcome. I am bored with the whole thing. I just want to go back to work.

The strike lasts sixteen days. The resorts are forced to kowtow to the union's demands. Once again, Bramlet's power has been proven.

However, for the state of Nevada and Clark County, the union strike causes such a severe loss of revenue that hundreds of employees are laid off. The consensus among the cocktail waitresses is that we feel we have been used, that something has been put over on us and no one can figure out exactly what.

But no matter; the strike is over, we had a good time, and on Tuesday, March 30 we're back to work. We still do not bother to pick up with regularity our paychecks, which are only a few pennies more than they were before.

The following month our union rep leaves the employ of Culinary Local 226 for a new, cushy job as MGM Grand Catering Manager.

The whole experience causes me to remember a line said by popular Las Vegas lounge comic Pete Barbutti: "Things would be much simpler if we had a Mafia President. The money could go direct to Sicily. It wouldn't have to go through labor unions."

\* \* \*

For Dor's birthday, the floormen in Pit Three buy her a thin, gold bracelet. Milton sees a gathering and hears laughter and approaches the pit to see what's happening. Dor has just secured the tiny clasp at her wrist.

"It's Dor's birthday," the pit boss tells Milton. "We gave her a bracelet."

At the end of the shift, Jane presents Dor with a pink warning slip for "wearing jewelry." Lenny stands in his doorway, the cigar in his mouth trembling with his excitement at this achievement.

Dor has received a previous "jewelry" warning notice for wearing a tiny St. Christopher medal. This was the same day that she came to work with a smudge on her forehead from a Catholic mass for Ash Wednesday. Even Lenny had the sense to not mention it on the warning notice—to let the smudge pass.

When Dor complained to the union about that warning notice, Bramlett told Lenny, "You can't tell people to take off religious medals."

Having made the point and to save face for the bar office, Dor had stopped wearing the little St. Christopher medal.

So this is Dor's second notice for the same infraction. She is officially fired.

Now, in order to get her job back, she is required to go to arbitration. Meanwhile, Bramlet gets her a job at the Las Vegas Hilton, where she wears a bikini and serves cocktails in the Vestal Virgin lounge.

It takes seven months for the arbitration date to be set. Besides Dor, Lenny, Milton, Bramlet, and an arbitrator, the MGM's legal counsel is present. Dor comes prepared with a lengthy written statement about everything she has experienced at the MGM leading up to her dismissal. She includes details of her harassment, and the fact that Lenny propositioned her.

Defense comes from Milton in the form of the accusation, "She told me to go fuck myself."

There's a break, and Bramlet is outside in the hallway with Dor. In a quiet voice he asks, "Did you really tell Milton Scafika to go fuck himself?"

Dor tosses her scarlet curls in disgust. She looks Bramlet straight in the eye and says, "Yes."

He touches her arm, guiding her further away from the door. "Did anybody hear you?"

"No."

"Good."

Back in the room, the arbitrator asks Dor, "Did you tell Milton Scafika to go fuck himself?"

Dor squints her eyes. "Do you think I would say such a thing like that?" Her back straightens in indignation.

To her amazement, they drop the subject.

Later she tells me, "Of course I would say such a thing like that, the stupid assholes. What was wrong with them? But I never denied it."

She wins the arbitration.

## CHAPTER 26 – Life decisions

My retired father stays for the rest of the summer. I hide from him and my husband the pain in my abdomen. I'm bloated with what I am sure is the beginning of my period. Since I began menstruating at twelve I have never been regular, so I never know exactly what to expect.

But these cramps are sharper and lasting longer than anything I've experienced before. The pain in my belly has progressed to the point where I can barely stand upright.

In the service bar diapering coffee glasses with napkins and rubber bands, I grimace from a sudden, searing stab in my belly. I can feel sweat on my forehead and in my armpits, and I double over to wait for the pain to subside.

Arline sets her tray down and begins to unload dirty glasses and empty ashtrays.

My breath is coming in gasps, and she turns to me with concern. "How often do you have bowel movements?" she asks.

"You get right to the point," I whisper. I am not sure I can stand up straight enough to fake being okay, but I continue to wrap those glasses like some kind of Stepford waitress.

"I'm serious." She begins to clean an ashtray with a napkin wet with lime juice. "You should have one every day. If not, you should give yourself an enema. Do you know Marilyn Monroe did enemas three times every day?"

I stop wrapping glasses to stare at her. "Why?"

"It's what actresses did in those days to keep their weight down."

I think of all the Marilyn impersonators in Las Vegas. Do they do this, too? How far would you go to be somebody else? I know guys who want to impersonate Elvis get plastic surgery—a surgeon friend of Del's counts sixteen of these procedures to date—so I guess three enemas a day isn't such a big sacrifice.

But I am not one of those children who grew up with a mother who gave you an enema every time you got sick. I'm not sure I would know how to do it. The bowel movement itself doesn't sound like a bad thing; if I had to choose between a bowel movement and an orgasm for the most satisfying release, I'm not sure I could.

I am also ready to try anything to relieve the pain I'm living with.

"The Egyptians invented the enema," Arline says.

Diane and Lily arrive at the bar bearing trays of dirty drink glasses.

Lily takes off her heart-shaped glasses and begins to clean them with a napkin. "You're talking about enemas? How gross."

"Hey," Diane says, "your father's a doctor. You shouldn't be bothered by gross."

"He's a *chiropractor*." Lily blinks her eyes and a puts her glasses back on.

Arline ignores them and continues. "The Egyptians watched the ibis—that's a bird with a long curled beak—take water into its beak and shove it up its ass and squirt it out."

"Eeeeuuuuw," Lily says.

Clap, clap. We all look toward the pit. The drink call is for Diane, who picks up her tray and leaves the service bar.

Arline says, "Carolyn, try an enema. It'll make you feel better. Like chicken soup, it can't hurt."

\* \* \*

The pain is constant now, a sharpness that cramps and clutches at my stomach. I have developed a hunched-over posture that makes me fear I'll soon walk like Rhonda. When I brush my teeth in the morning, I gag on my toothpaste.

In the dressing room, as I change out of my uniform, Karen looks at me and says, "How far along are you?"

"What?" I have no idea what she's talking about.

"You're pregnant, aren't you?"

Pregnant? I chill at the thought. "I don't think so. I mean, I have no idea."

Since I was nineteen I have used either birth control pills or a diaphragm, and at thirty-one, I have never been pregnant. For six months I have been wearing a contraceptive intrauterine device (IUD) called the Dalkon Shield, aggressively marketed worldwide in 1974 by the A.H. Robins Company as the newest, safest and most reliable birth control method available. How can I possibly be pregnant?

I don't waste any time. I get on the phone and manage to squeeze in an appointment for the next day with my gynecologist.

The test and Dr. Ames confirm that I am indeed pregnant. He tells me the presence of the Dalkon Shield explains the chronic pain I am experiencing.

This pain tells me instinctively that there is something very wrong with this pregnancy. I don't even consider having the baby. Dear God, no way could I live with this pain for another seven months!

"It's probable," says Dr. Ames, "that, because of the IUD, you will miscarry."

Before I leave the office I make an appointment for a D&C— the politically correct abortion term—on Thursday, my next day off. I just want this excruciating pain to stop. Dr. Ames agrees to remove the IUD at the same time. The cost for the procedure is $150.

"We'll need the full amount, in advance, in cash," his nurse informs me.

Driving home, I think about the baby growing inside me. I put my hand on my stomach and try to feel some sense of communing with it. I try to imagine it as a real person, but I can't. I can't get past the pain. Can it be in pain, as well?

One other thing disturbs me: I can't be sure who the father is.

For the first time, I see the dark side to the life I have been leading as a Las Vegas cocktail waitress. Is this the price I will have to pay? I feel shame that my happy-go-lucky, promiscuous behavior has resulted in the beginning of this new life.

That evening at dinner I say little. How can I tell my father I am going to have an abortion? I give silent thanks that my mother is not alive to witness this.

Later in the evening, after my father has retired and Del and I are alone in our bedroom, I say, "I have something to tell you."

"You and Ronni want to go shopping again in LA," he jokes.

"I'm pregnant," I say.

He stares at me.

"It's not right. I'm in terrible pain and I think it's because of the IUD. I've scheduled an abortion for Thursday."

"What?" He throws his gun belt across the room, and it crashes against the baseboard at the bottom of the wall.

I am stunned by his reaction.

"You're having an *abortion*?" he hisses. We are keeping our voices down so as not awaken my father. "You can't do that. I'm *Catholic* and abortion's against my religion."

Since we never go to church and seldom have occasion to talk about religion, I get the impression that he is Catholic when it's convenient, when it supports his views.

"Well, I'm *not* Catholic and I need to get rid of this. Besides, before we got married, you said you didn't want to have children. I agreed to that. That's why I have the damned Dalkon Shield in the first place." It's hard to keep my voice down. "What did you think we'd do if I got pregnant?" I begin to cry.

"I never thought about it," he mumbles. "Guess I assumed you'd just have it."

"Well, I'm *not* going to just have it. This pregnancy isn't right. I can't stand the pain."

Recovered from his initial shock, he retorts, "You can't have an abortion because it's not legal."

"What?"

"I said, it's not legal."

"Yes, it is. Roe versus Wade made it legal last year in a landmark Supreme Court decision."

He stares at me. "I didn't know that."

Aghast, I say, "You work for a judge! One of the most controversial political and legal changes in this country, debated all over TV and radio and in the newspapers, and you *missed* it?"

Del does not give up easily. "If it's so *legal*, why does the doctor want his hundred and fifty dollars up front?"

I have the quick answer. "Because I am a cocktail waitress," I snap, "and he is afraid I'll change my mind. He's afraid he'll get stiffed if he does it before he's paid."

Del starts to talk about how I—he never says *we*—should have the child. He has completely forgotten the part about my pain. In this moment I hate him for his machismo, Catholic attitude.

I beg him not to say anything to or in front of my father. I have never had any intimate conversation with my father. I would be mortified, my father would be frightened for my safety, and I would feel guilty for alarming him.

I am firm in my decision. For the next two days a strained mood permeates the house. Del manifests his disapproval with silence. I tell Dad that my husband is under a lot of stress in his job. With constant pain in my abdomen, I struggle to move normally. My father senses something is wrong, but he doesn't ask questions.

I never tell my husband that I can't be sure who the father of this baby is.

* * *

On Thursday, April 25, 1976 after Del has gone to work, I tell my father I am going shopping and to have lunch with Arline at the Boulevard Mall. She will pick me up at 9 a.m. and I won't be back till mid-afternoon. "That way we only have to drive one car."

I think of all the horror stories I have heard about women who have been forced to choose an illegal abortion in a basement, in a back room, or across the border in Mexico. I take a Valium, so I'm not nervous. I look forward to the relief of having a pain-free body, of again being able to stand erect.

Nobody in Dr. Ames' office treats me any different from if I had come for an annual pap smear. The procedure goes well and in an hour, it is done. I am so grateful that I am able to go to a doctor and have this done in a safe, sterile environment, with no fear of legal repercussions. Thank you, U.S. Supreme Court.

I lean on Arline as we leave and walk to her car. Woozy from the anesthesia, I feel no pain. Sitting inside the car, my body now feels heavy and tired. But not too tired to go to lunch.

"Let's go to Chateau Vegas," Arline says.

"Fine." Nothing like a nice glass of white wine—or two—to extend the afterglow of anesthesia.

Two hours later, when Arline drops me off at home, I am blotto.

"I had a lot to drink at lunch and I'm really sleepy," I tell my dad. "I'm going in to take a nap."

For the rest of the afternoon this light bulb is out.

At 5 p.m. I get up and begin to pull stuff out of the refrigerator to cook dinner. Both anesthesia and wine have worn off, and I ache, so I take a Tylenol. With my mind on automatic pilot I prepare dinner for my father and Del.

That night when we go to bed Del does not ask about my day. He is pleasant enough, but he doesn't even ask how I feel. He acts as if the pregnancy and abortion never happened.

The next day I am back at the MGM on the floor promptly at 11 a.m. to begin my shift.

Del respects my wish to say nothing to my father; we never again discuss the abortion.

* * *

Some of the cocktail waitresses and bartenders have formed a dinner club. Every week someone cooks dinner at their house for about twelve people. The food prepared is based on interest or ethnic origin. My heritage is German, but two weeks ago, a Hungarian waitress served German food. Since Del's heritage is Polish, I serve Stuffed Cabbage and Chicken Paprikash.

Bartender Kevin has just gotten engaged to a young blonde named Kathy. She doesn't work in the hotel, but has met a lot of his friends. Kevin brings her to my dinner, along with a couple of bottles of champagne to celebrate their engagement.

Kevin and Kathy have been living together for a year. When this subject comes up in the presence of my father, I am not sure how he'll react. I think living together before you get married is something new to my sixties' generation.

My father surprises me. His smile is gentle. "I understand how it is today," he says. "I know people my age who are living together without being married because it's better tax-wise."

For a warm and fuzzy moment I consider that later I might tell him about my abortion. Then a voice in my head asks, "Why, when you know it will only hurt him?"

A painful vision enters my head: When I was thirteen he caught me and two girlfriends sitting in the back yard lawn swing in the dark, smoking cigarettes. Instead of punishing me, he said, "Your mother and I are very disappointed in you." The look on his face and the emotion in his voice were enough to shame me into the ground. I never smoked again.

No, I won't ever tell him about the abortion. I don't ever again want to see that look.

## CHAPTER 27 – Values lost and found

Friday is Arline's birthday. A great excuse for Girls' Night Out. The day before, I inform Del that I won't be home Friday night till late.

Lara, Ronni, Diane, Arline and I spend the day planning our evening.

After work we head over to the Village Pub, where we know all the bartenders who work there.

"Champagne cocktails all around," Ronni says. "We're celebrating Arline's birthday." This bartender is smart enough not to ask how old Arline is.

From the Village Pub we drive down Eastern to the Coachmen's Inn for dinner. A popular steak joint, we know all the bartenders there, too. Ronni switches to vodka on the rocks, and the rest of us order more champagne cocktails. With dinner we consume two bottles of red wine.

Of course, we don't pay for any of these drinks or dinner— everyone loves to see the MGM girls. We "decorate" these places. One of the girls recently had her picture appear, just like a celebrity, in *Panorama* when she—"an MGM cocktail waitress"— was seen dining at the Copa Lounge. And of course we are known to tip well.

From there we are off to the Casbah Lounge at the Sahara to catch The Treniers, then on to the Aladdin showroom, where Ronni's husband comps us into the 2 a.m. show.

A nightcap or three later, it's five in the morning. I stand under the Aladdin's *porte cochère* waiting for my car, tottering on my stiletto sandals. In my left hand I carry a stinger on the rocks, and in my right hand I hold my valet claim ticket and a few dollars to tip the valet attendant.

Because I'm drunk and not paying attention, I give the tip with the ticket to the attendant who runs for the car. I'm not thinking about the fact that a different attendant will actually bring around the car.

The Caddy comes, I finish off the Stinger, leave the glass on the valet desk, and totter to the car. The attendant holds the door open and I climb in. I put my purse on the seat beside me. He closes the door, glowers at me through the open window and mutters, "I'll pass your thanks on to my landlady."

In a flash, he is running back to the valet stand. I am out of the car, furious. I may be drunk, but not too drunk to climb onto the front seat, lean over the top of the car, and shriek in his direction, *"You fucking asshole! I gave the fucking tip to your fucking partner!"*

I climb back into the Caddy and peel out of the driveway, muttering to myself about how fucking stupid fucking valet attendants are.

* * *

For several sober days I am haunted by the image I must have presented at the valet at the Aladdin. I can still hear myself shrieking obscenities at the parking attendant. When did I turn into some kind of creature I don't respect, let alone like? I feel cheap—hard in a way that, if they knew, would cause my parents to feel painful disappointment.

How did everything get so weird? It feels like while I am having a wild Disney E-ride in the bright lights of Las Vegas, everything around me is falling into darkness. I will get off the rollercoaster to discover I am alone and the park is closed and empty.

My marriage is rocky. Del loves the money I make, but he doesn't hide the fact that he has no respect for cocktail waitresses. I think about what it would be like to have a regular job that would match his work schedule, where we would have the same days off and be able to do more things together.

I think about getting back into graphic design. I imagine the world of advertising to be more sane—certainly more respectable—than the world of casino gaming.

If I have lost my self-respect and my dignity, does it matter how much money I make? Maybe by changing my lifestyle I can get the real me back. Maybe by changing my lifestyle I can save my marriage.

A week later, on May 23, 1976, I walk into the bar office at the end of my shift and give Lenny my notice to quit the MGM.

* * *

## EPILOGUE – 38 years later

**Carlos and Theresa Farfan** formed Circus de Carlo, which played the parking lot at Sam's Town for several years before going bankrupt for inept management. Armando and his family went back to work for Ringling Brothers. Today Armando's sons Tato and Gino work in technical fields for Cirque Du Soleil.

After May Advertising went under, **Jerry May** resurfaced as Southwest Advertising. Along with Martin Black, marketing director of the Stardust, he got into trouble for submitting invoices to the hotel with fake full-page *San Diego Tribune* ad tear sheets. The way the scam worked was the money from the hotel for the newspaper ad placements was able to be pocketed because the ads were never actually purchased. I always wondered where Jerry and Martin had those phony tear sheets produced. Full-page newspaper presses in Las Vegas were the *Review-Journal*, the *Las Vegas Sun* and—Bob Brown's *Valley Times*. The Stardust's mob management did not take this deception well. Jerry May left town suddenly. Martin Black went to prison, where he subsequently died.

Jerry's partner, **Jim Joyce**, joined Marydean Martin in 1975 to found Joyce and Martin Advertising. His clever political campaign strategies helped elect so many legislators that he was considered the most effective lobbyist ever seen in the state Capitol. In 1993 he died of pneumonia brought on by emphysema.

In 1977, after refusing to pay for the Starboard Tack and Village Pub car bombs he ordered because they didn't blow, **Al Bramlet's** naked body was found in a shallow desert grave near Mount Potosi. **Tom Hanley** shot him six times, including once in each ear. Cops gossiped that his son Gramby shot him "right in the balls." Hanley and his son were convicted of Bramlet's murder and sentenced to life. Tom Hanley died in prison. Gramby Hanley disappeared into the Federal Witness Protection Program, emerging briefly in 1982 to testify before a U.S. Senate panel investigating illegal union activities. Ronni said Gramby was actually an accomplished artist; who knows what great—legitimate—career he might have had?

In a fraudulent election, **Ben Schmoutey** took over Al Bramlet's position as General Secretary at the Culinary Union. The death of popular Bramlet cost the union thirty percent of its membership.

Shortly after **James Ray Houston's** casino visit, he was exposed by the *Las Vegas Sun* newspaper for operating a fraudulent mail-order gold-and-silver business. He was not elected governor.

In the summer of 1977 Del and I divorced when he turned 50 and gave up sex for chewing tobacco.

The intrauterine contraceptive, **Dalkon Shield**, was not removed, as we had agreed, by Dr. Ames during my abortion. Five years later the resulting pelvic inflammatory disease and total hysterectomy won me a significant settlement against Dr. Ames and the Dalkon Shield's manufacturer, A.H. Robbins.

**Arline** developed a brain tumor and in 1977 died at home in Phoenix with her family. Ronni said Arline died because "she didn't want to be forty."

After twelve years **Ronni** left the MGM, went back to UNLV, got Bachelor's and Master's degrees, and now heads up a history research department at a major university.

**Lara** was last seen working as a cocktail waitress in the blackjack pit at Harrah's Hotel & Casino.

After they got drunk and quit the MGM, **Lily** became a successful State Farm insurance agent. She did not stay friends with **Rhonda**.

**Mariella** was last seen dealing blackjack at the Rio Hotel & Casino.

**Dor** saved her money and bought a little cowboy bar in Boulder City, Nevada.

**Alice** married Lenny and was last seen volunteering as a candy-striper at Sunrise Hospital.

**Lenny** was fired from the MGM when he was caught at the back door stealing liquor and hams.

The **Las Vegas Celebrity Train** never completed its "inaugural run." Another attempt at what Las Vegans call "the bullet train" was made in the mid 1980s, with an actual train full of dignitaries and VIPs going as far as Jean, Nevada and back. Then again, nothing. It is said that the reason a successful bullet train has never been completed is that some of the money to pay for it would have to come from the State of California, which is not interested in financing transportation for weekend vacations that take money into another state.

In 1986 **Kirk Kerkorian** sold the MGM Grand Las Vegas to Bally Manufacturing, which somehow got rid of all those decorative lions and renamed the hotel, Bally's.

**Jeff Silver** became the man in charge of the Las Vegas Office for the Nevada State Gaming Control Board. He became Chairman of the Greater Las Vegas Chamber of Commerce, and President of the Riviera Hotel & Casino. Today he is Chairman of the Gaming and Administrative Law Department of the legal firm Gordon/Silver and is authorized to practice law before all Nevada courts, the U.S. Tax court, the U.S. District Court for Nevada and the United States Supreme Court. He still plays the harmonica.

From 1979 to 1986 **Bob Miller** served as Clark County District Attorney. He was then elected Lieutenant Governor, and became acting governor in 1989 when Governor Richard Bryan was elected to the U.S. Senate. From 1990 to 1998 he and Sandy served as Governor and First Lady. Sandy Miller became the second First

Lady to give birth while living in Carson City's Governor's Mansion.

In September, 1991 **Paul Goldman** was killed in an auto accident on the two-lane highway to Pahrump, Nevada.

**Lieutenant Governor Harry Reid** became a major force of the Democratic Party and today serves as the United States Senate Majority Leader.

**Teddy Binion** died September 17, 1998 of a cocktail combination of black tar heroin and the sedative Xanax, forcefully administered by his stripper girlfriend, Sandy Murphy and her trucker boyfriend Rick Tabish. The homicide became a high profile trial in Nevada, televised on Court TV. The two received life sentences that were later overturned on a technicality by the Nevada Supreme Court. In 2008 their story was produced by Lifetime television as a movie called "*Sex and Lies in Sin City: the Ted Binion Scandal.*"

After nine years at the MGM, our first cocktail waiter, **Jimmy Henderson** and his partner moved to San Francisco, where Jimmy acted in a dinner theater. They later moved back to Las Vegas. Jimmy just recently passed away.

The northwest corner of Tropicana and the Strip was sold and the **Lone Palm Motel & Trailer Park** was razed. The New York, New York Hotel/Casino opened on the spot in 1997.

**The Stardust** was imploded at 2:30 a.m. March 13, 2007.

According to their culinary union contract, when Bally's bought the MGM Grand, MGM cocktail waitresses had to be retained with the highest seniority. Five original girls, including **Jayda** and **Betty**—now in their sixties—still work cocktails at Bally's.

-THE END-

**Thanks for reading *Coming to Las Vegas!***

## Reviews are everything!
If you enjoyed this book, I would really appreciate it if you would go to Amazon, rate the book and write one or two lines about what you liked about my story.

## *Carolyn*
www.carolynvhamilton.com

## GROUP GUIDE

### Please recommend *Coming to Las Vegas* to your reading group.

Here are some questions you might want to discuss:

1 – What was your favorite scene in the story?

2 – With which person in the story did you feel the most "connection?"

3 – What do you think about how Las Vegas has changed over the years?

4 – Have you ever worked as a cocktail waitress? Was it a good experience, or an unpleasant experience?

5 – What do you think about casino work as viable employment? Do you think it would be possible to have a "normal" family life with such a job?

6 – Do you think it would be exciting to live and work in Las Vegas?

7 – What part of the story did you think was most bizarre?

8 – How do you feel about sexism in the workplace?

9 – Have you ever felt any kind of unusual pressure in the workplace because you are a woman? Or a man?

Other books by Carolyn V. Hamilton:

## FICTION

### *MAGICIDE*
### *(a murder mystery)*

Maxwell Beacham-Jones, the world's most famous magician, has reached the zenith of his success. Now he's planned the most daring, outrageous trick of his career.

But when Maxwell dies in a Las Vegas roller coaster escape stunt before a national television audience, it's no accident. He was hated by his contemporaries, and all of the suspects are magicians—with plenty of secret motives for murder.

MAGICIDE introduces Las Vegas Metro Police detective and single mom, Cheri Raymer, and her vegetarian partner, Tony Pizzarelli. Together they follow a trail through the world of magic and show business that leads to intrigue and shocking revelations.

Raymer will face the most devastating personal threat in her career when her teen-aged son, Tom, fascinated by magic, becomes the protégé of a suspected killer.

### *HARD AMAZON RAIN*
### *(An eco-adventure romance)*

Burned-out art therapist Dianti Robertson dreams of building a library for an Amerindian village on the upper Amazon in Peru. She's searching for a feeling of completion, and the library is a project completely different from her ongoing work with troubled children in America.

Roaming the the Amazon River, English eco-activist Christian St. Cloud sails his trimaran, the *Rio Vida*, wherever he perceives a threat to the Amerindian way of life, opposing those whose greed would strip the people of all their natural resources. Christian is haunted by having been unable to save nine indigenous villages from being destroyed by a dam project in Venezuela.

Dianti and Christian strongly disagree on how best to aid indigenous people. Complicating their outspoken differences is the intensity of their unspoken physical attraction.

Dutch soldier-of-fortune Kees Wijntuin and a ruthless gold consortium threaten the area where Dianti lives. When two young Amerindians are kidnapped by the Dutchman and sold into slavery at the mining camp of Santo Ignacio, Dianti and Christian must join forces to rescue them.

### *ELIZABETH SAMSON, FORBIDDEN BRIDE*
### *(a historical fiction based on a true story)*

In the 18th century Dutch plantation colony of Suriname, where wealth is measured by the number of slaves one owns, the Free Negress Elisabeth Samson, educated and wealthy owner of several flourishing coffee plantations, wants only to marry her true love, a white man.

But can she overcome the strict Dutch laws forbidding marriage between black and white against the powerful forces of the colonial Governor, the white planters who make up the Court of Justice, and the Society of Suriname, who call her whore, covet her property, and accuse her of treason?

**WATCH FOR**
# IMPLOSION
**TO DEBUT FALL 2015**

With the pending implosion of the grand old Las Vegas hotel/casino, the Desert Palace, an eleven-year-old mystery of six million dollars stolen from the casino count room remains unsolved.

Everyone who has touched the money has died a horrible death, giving rise to the legend that this money is cursed.

Newspaper reporter Nedra Dean feels the pressure to use every means she can to make this dramatic moment in Las Vegas history her biggest scoop, one she hopes will catapult her to big-time journalism at CNN.

Celebrity maitre d' Eduardo only wants to reconcile his estranged family before his forced retirement.

And somewhere, within the walls and floors of the Desert Palace, the cursed six million dollars waits, which owner "Crazy" Foxy Craig is desperate to find before the walls come tumbling down.

## AUTOBIOGRAPHY

### *MY MIND IS AN OPEN MOUTH*
With his outlandish, machine-gun rapid-fire humor, comedian Cork Proctor has been knockin' 'em dead for sixty years … literally. From his first attempt at stand-up comedy as a gravedigger entertaining his co-worker to lounges and showrooms around the world — on land and sea — this left-handed, dyslexic, two-time high school dropout has not only seen it all, he tells it all.

### PRAISE FOR MY MIND IS AN OPEN MOUTH:

*Sit up, take a deep breath, pat down your hair, and straighten your tie. Cork Proctor is known for playing with the audience.*
        **—Dick Clark, Television Host**

*Roastmaster General of the United States.*

**—Tip O'Neill, former Speaker of the House**

*Cork Proctor has been one of the funniest men in Las Vegas for many glowing years. Read his book: Giggle and laugh!*
**—Phyllis Diller, Comedienne**

*The fastest, funniest comedic mind and mouth in town.*
**— Las Vegas Sun**

*His observations are intelligent, his delivery original. He is in command at all times, and like the drums he plays, his mind works in a double paradiddle beat. In other words, I like him: Brash, bright, and brilliant!*
**—Shecky Greene, Comedian**

* * *

www.ingramcontent.com/pod-product-compliance
Lightning Source LLC
Chambersburg PA
CBHW071336090426
42738CB00012B/2917